God
Made
You
YOU!

Jean Fischer

God Made You YOU!

Devotions for Girls

BARBOUR **kidz**

A Division of Barbour Publishing

ISBN 978-1-63609-926-2

Published by Barbour Publishing, Inc., 1810 Barbour Drive, Uhrichsville, Ohio 44683, www.barbourbooks.com

Our mission is to inspire the world with the life-changing message of the Bible.

Member of the
Evangelical Christian
Publishers Association

Printed in China.

002128 0824 HA

INTRODUCTION

Life is an ever-changing adventure. Each day holds something exciting to discover and learn.

As you travel through life, you will grow and change. How you look will change, and so will your thoughts, hopes, and dreams. You will learn new things about yourself and meet new friends along the way. Some will stay with you, and others will choose a different path through life. There is one friend, though, you can always count on—one who will never leave you. He is God, and He created you.

The same God who created the universe made YOU! He designed you with special gifts and purpose. Do you wonder how God sees you and why He made you? The devotions in this book will help you understand. As you read and think about each one and its accompanying scripture verse, God will open your eyes to who you are and who He wants you to be.

WHO AM I?

For You made the parts inside me.
You put me together inside my mother.
PSALM 139:13

Let's start with a question. Who are you? Maybe you answered with just your name. Your name identifies you, but you are way more than what you're called. You are a unique, one-of-a-kind girl created by God.

Long before you were born, God knew you. He designed your character—your personality. He decided what you would look like and who your parents would be. When He was ready God put all the parts together and He made you YOU! He gave you life.

No one on earth is exactly like you. When you look in the mirror you see yourself on the outside. But you are much more than what you see. You can be kind, funny, caring, thankful, helpful, friendly, generous, and dependable. God also gave you special skills and talents—the things you are good at. So, answer the question again. Who are you? What makes you one of a kind?

. . . .

Dear God, show me who I am. Show me who You made me to Be. Amen.

MADE IN HIS IMAGE

And God made man in His own likeness. In the likeness of God He made him. He made both male and female.
GENESIS 1:27

No one knows what God looks like, but we know a lot about His personality. By reading the Bible, we learn about His character—the things that make God GOD. We know He is caring, trustworthy, patient, kind, forgiving, generous, and truthful. God loves us all the time, even when we disobey and do things that make Him sad. He is helpful and always wants the best for us.

When God created us, He made us in His image—to reflect who He is. He put inside us the ability to be good in many of the ways He is good. God made us to share parts of His personality. We aren't exactly like God because He is so much more than we ever could be. But in some ways we are like Him. Can you name a few ways your personality is like God's?

Dear God, You created me to be good the way You are good. I'm glad You made me to be like You. Amen.

I AM A CHILD OF GOD

*See what great love the Father has for us
that He would call us His children.*
1 JOHN 3:1

When God made you, He was pleased with His creation. He loved His special, one-of-a-kind girl. God loved you then, He loves you now, and He will love you forever.

God plans to stay super-involved in your life. He will never leave you or let you down. Another name for God is "our heavenly Father." He says, "I will be a Father to you. You will be My sons and daughters" (read it in your Bible, 2 Corinthians 6:18). You are a child of God. He loves you with a special, indescribable, perfect kind of love.

Although you can't see God with your eyes, your heavenly Father is with you every minute of every day guiding and helping you. As you learn more about who He is and how much He loves you, your relationship with God will get even stronger. You can learn about God by reading your Bible and also by talking with people who know and love Him.

Dear heavenly Father, help me to know You better. Teach me to trust and depend on You. Amen.

TALKING WITH GOD

Never stop praying.
1 THESSALONIANS 5:17

Imagine living with your dad yet neither of you speaks to the other, ever! That's a silly thought, isn't it? Talking is how people communicate.

Prayer is how you communicate with God. It's how you tell your heavenly Father your thoughts and what you want and need. And it's how you thank Him for all the wonderful things He does for you. There is no one right way to pray. Your words don't have to be fancy, but they should be respectful.

You can talk with God all the time. You don't have to pray out loud. You can talk with God silently in your thoughts. You can tell Him anything, even those things you worry about or are ashamed of. Remember, God loves you! If you've messed up, He won't be angry with you, punish you, leave you, or love you less.

Get in the habit of talking with Him all day long. The more you communicate with God, the better you will know Him. He will help you to know yourself better too.

Hello, God, it's me. Let's talk awhile....

MY BEST FRIEND, JESUS

*"I call you friends, because I have told you
everything I have heard from My Father."*
JOHN 15:15

Maybe you already know about God's Son, Jesus. Jesus was there when God created you. He knows you as well as God the Father does—because They are one!

Long ago, God the Father sent Jesus to earth to live with us for a while. Jesus taught us to love, trust, and obey God. He set the perfect example of how God wants us to live. When God created you, He gave you a purpose—actually, more than one. But your main purpose is to become more like Jesus. You can read about Him in your Bible in the books of Matthew, Mark, Luke, and John. Pay attention to what Jesus said and taught and also how He behaved and interacted with others. Think about ways you can become more like Him.

Jesus is your best friend! He understands what it's like to be human. Through His Holy Spirit He is with you all the time, ready to help with whatever you need. Jesus loves you as much as God the Father does. You can talk with Him just like you talk with God.

Dear Jesus, my Best friend, teach me
to Become more like you. Amen.

GOD HAS PLANS FOR ME

"For I know the plans I have for you," says the Lord, "plans for well-being and not for trouble, to give you a future and a hope."
JEREMIAH 29:11

"What do you want to be when you grow up?" You've probably been asked that question a gazillion times.

God already knows what's ahead for you. He has plans for your whole life. He put you on earth for a special reason. When God created you, He gave you skills and talents you can use to serve Him. If you follow His plan, God will help you use those skills and talents to make the world a better place.

Maybe your purpose is to serve God in a humongous way that the whole world will notice. Or your purpose might be to work in a quiet but powerful way behind the scenes. Whatever He wants you to do, God's plan is perfect. He's already put inside you the desire to learn what you're good at, and gradually He will reveal more of His plan for you. Ask God to lead you, then listen for His guidance.

Dear God, how can I serve You? Guide me toward Your perfect plan. Amen.

GOD WATCHES OVER ME

But now this is what the LORD says, who created you. . ."Do not fear, for I have redeemed you. I have called you by your name. You are Mine."
ISAIAH 43:1 SKJV

Go outside and look at the stars. God made each one and gave it a name (Psalm 147:4). Even before your parents named you, God knew *your* name. He knows in advance every detail of your life, including little things like when you'll stand up and sit down (Psalm 139:2), how many hairs are on your head (Matthew 10:30), and what you'll think before you think it (Psalm 139:2).

God sees you not only today but in the future as well. He already knows if you will get married, what you'll look like on your wedding day, and the names of your husband and children.

Maybe you feel uncomfortable that God knows all about you and is always watching you. But He isn't spying on you, trying to catch you doing something wrong. He is doing what every good father does—watching over His little girl and making sure she's okay.

Father, I feel special knowing you love me and watch over me. Amen.

13

I CAN TRUST GOD

But as for me, I trust in You, O Lord.
I say, "You are my God."
PSALM 31:14

Is there someone you trust completely to always be good and honest, and never to hurt you? It's wonderful having people you can trust. But no one is perfect. Everyone messes up sometimes, and those mess-ups can hurt and get in the way of us trusting each other.

God is the only one who is perfectly trustworthy. He never messes up. God created you to trust Him. You can trust Him to always be with you, to strengthen you (especially when you feel weak and afraid), to have a good plan for your life, to answer your prayers, to meet your needs, to love you deeply, and to forgive you no matter what. You can trust God to always be ready to fight for you. You belong to Him, and He will never let you down.

Dear God, thank You for loving and caring for me. You are the one I can trust all the time, no matter what. Help me to trust You with all of my heart. Amen.

GOD IS FAITHFUL

Now faith is being sure we will get what we hope for. It is being sure of what we cannot see.

HEBREWS 11:1

You can trust God 100 percent, but He didn't expect you would trust Him completely right away. Trust is something you build one step at a time.

When you were little, you learned to trust your parents. If you were unsure or scared, you grabbed your mom's or dad's hand and held it tight. That connection made you feel safe. You learned you could have faith in your parents to hold on to you and not let go.

That's the kind of relationship God wants with you. Whenever you are uncertain or afraid, you can imagine Him holding your hand and keeping you safe. In time, you will discover God is always faithful to love and protect you. His faithfulness will help you increase your faith in Him. Faith is more than hoping God is with you. It is being sure He will take good care of you no matter what.

Dear God, Build my faith in You. Show me You are always with me, keeping me safe. Amen.

15

MY SPECIAL GIFTS

There are different kinds of gifts. But it is the same Holy Spirit Who gives them. There are different kinds of work to be done for Him. But the work is for the same Lord. There are different ways of doing His work. But it is the same God who uses all these ways in all people.

1 CORINTHIANS 12:4–6

God gives everyone different gifts, things they are good at. What are your special gifts?

Maybe you are a talented singer, dancer, musician, artist, or actor. You might be good at sports, crafts, baking, writing, science, math, or building and fixing things. You are super-skilled in other ways too, ways unique to your character—your personality. Maybe you are good at caring for family members when they're sick, cheering people up when they're sad, taking care of animals, or helping whenever you see a need.

How you use your gifts is unique to you. No one does things exactly like you do. You should use your gifts in ways that please God.

Heavenly Father, thank You for giving me things I am good at. Teach me to use my gifts well. Amen.

REACH FOR THE STARS!

Be strong with the Lord's strength.
EPHESIANS 6:10

Is there something you really, *really* want to do, but you think you can't? Maybe you worry you're not good enough or strong enough. The Bible says Jesus gives us strength to do those things we think are impossible.

Strength doesn't necessarily mean building up your muscles. It's more about the way we think. You should set your goals and reach for the stars, but don't think you will reach your goals all at once. It takes time. Ask Jesus to help you do your best and to stay positive when things get hard. Ask Him to help you try again whenever you fail.

If you doubt yourself or feel weak, remember that God can make you strong. Keep your eyes on your goal—and even more importantly, keep your eyes on Jesus. Put your faith and trust in Him. If you're headed to where He wants you to go, Jesus will help you get there.

. . . .

Dear Jesus, you know the goals I want to reach. Lead me. Guide me. Give me some of your strength so I can keep going even when it's hard. Amen.

LOST IN SPACE

"What if one of you had one hundred sheep and you lost one of them? Would you not leave the ninety-nine in the country and go back and look for the one which was lost until you find it?"

LUKE 15:4

What if instead of having a goal and reaching for the stars, you don't know what you want to do? What if you don't know which of your interests to follow or you're searching for something so interesting it's all you'd ever think about?

You aren't alone; we all have those "lost in space" kinds of feelings when we don't know exactly what we want. When you feel that way, talk with Jesus about it. Ask Him to guide you.

If you were really lost, Jesus would search for you. He would find you wherever you were and lead you where He wants you to go. Jesus knows you better than anyone else. Ask Him to help you find your way. He already knows where you should go, and you can trust Him to guide you there.

Dear Jesus, please lead me to things that excite me, things I'll be passionate about. Amen.

18

YOUR ULTIMATE GOAL

*Let us keep running in the race that
God has planned for us.*

HEBREWS 12:1

Your "ultimate goal" is the one thing that's most important to you. You will have many dreams in your life, but your ultimate goal should be pleasing God.

In your own power, you can never 100 percent please Him. (You'd need to be perfect to do that, and no one except God is perfect.) But you should try your best. Think of life as a race to the finish line. Someday when your life is done, you will meet God face-to-face. You'll want to tell Him, "I did my best."

The race won't be easy. Along the way life will give you hills and valleys, bumps, twists, and turns. But remember you aren't running the race alone. Jesus is alongside you, encouraging you, helping you to keep on running. If you get tired and feel like giving up, then imagine Jesus picking you up and carrying you. He is your trusted partner in the race. The two of you will run it together.

Dear Jesus. I'm ready to start. Let's go! Amen.

PRACTICE, PRACTICE, PRACTICE

You know that only one person gets a crown for being in a race even if many people run. You must run so you will win the crown.
1 CORINTHIANS 9:24

Imagine a gymnastics competition where some of the girls had never practiced. You'd know who they were because they'd mess up, trip, fall. . .maybe even hurt themselves. There's no way they will win a trophy. Winning takes practice.

Serious athletes work hard. They eat well, get enough rest, and focus on building strength. They also practice self-control. They learn to avoid anything that separates them from reaching their goals. Self-control is most important as you work toward your ultimate goal of pleasing God. Every day you should practice avoiding those things that displease and separate you from God, things like disobeying your parents, lying, and being selfish or unkind.

As you practice behaving to please God, you might not always win the prize—but you will always win at doing your best and setting a good example for others.

Dear God, teach me to behave in ways that please you. Help me to set a good example. Amen.

20

MY INSIDE VOICE

Your ears will hear a word behind you,
saying, "This is the way, walk in it," whenever
you turn to the right or to the left.
ISAIAH 30:21

When God made you, He gave you a voice so you could talk and sing. He also gave you an inside voice—your conscience. It's God's voice telling you what's right and what's wrong.

You might not always know if a certain behavior is pleasing to God. If you're unsure, stop and listen. You won't hear God speaking aloud to you, but you will sense His voice speaking inside your heart. God's voice is kind but firm. If you feel Him saying, "No!" then it's time to rethink your behavior.

When you feel good about how you're behaving and you're following God's directions in the Bible, it's most likely God saying, "Yes!" Sometimes you will sense other voices speaking inside your heart, trying to lead you in the wrong direction or make you feel not good enough or confused. Don't listen to them! Ask God to help you recognize His voice among the others.

Dear God, help me to know Your voice speaking inside my heart. Amen.

BEHAVIOR CHECKUP

*Put yourselves through a test. See if you belong
to Christ. Then you will know you belong to
Christ, unless you do not pass the test.*
2 CORINTHIANS 13:5

It's time for a checkup. Take a few minutes right now to list all the wonderful behaviors that make you YOU!

Think about the ways you behave that are pleasing to God. Are you kind, respectful, friendly, cooperative, or generous? Add them to your list. Keep adding to your list even small things like smiling at others or holding the door open for them. When you've finished listing all the good behaviors you can think of, thank God for filling you up with all that awesomeness! As you get to know Him better and your relationship with Him grows stronger, you will add even more things to the list.

Next, list behaviors you'd like to improve. Maybe you're just a little bit bossy, impatient, or careless. It's okay. Everyone needs some improvement. No one is perfect after all! Ask God to help you change those behaviors.

Father God, thank You for helping me be good
and to become even better. Amen.

PLAY BY THE RULES

*Anyone who runs in a race must follow
the rules to get the crown.*
2 TIMOTHY 2:5

Rules are everywhere. When you run a race or play a game, there are rules to follow. Every household has rules too. What are the rules at your house?

Parents set rules about their kids' bedtime, homework, screen time, what they can watch on TV, where they can go, who they can hang out with. . . The list of rules might seem endless. Maybe you are unhappy with some of your parents' rules and wonder why they made them. But your parents set rules because they love you. Respecting their rules will help you stay safe and also guide you in becoming the best *you* you can be.

Like every good parent, our heavenly Father makes rules for us to follow. God loves you. You are His child. Respecting His rules will help you get along well with others and grow up to be an even better person than you are right now—a person who's more like Jesus.

Dear God, thank You for reminding me to respect my parent's rules and Your rules too. Amen.

CHOOSE TO OBEY

"So obey the Lord your God. Keep all of His Laws which I tell you today."
DEUTERONOMY 27:10

God is pleased when we obey His rules. When He created us, God gave us freedom to choose our behavior. We can choose to follow His rules or not.

From the beginning of time, people chose not to follow God's rules. Disobeying His rules is called sin. The first humans, Adam and Eve, were the first people to sin. God gave them a lovely garden to live in, and they had just one rule: "Do not eat the fruit from that one special tree." Adam and Eve chose to do what they wanted instead. They ate the fruit. They sinned—messed up—and there were consequences. Instead of choosing the good path through life that God had planned for them, they chose a path leading to trouble and sadness. (Read more about it in Genesis 3.)

While racing toward your goals, you will be more successful if you follow God's rules in the Bible.

Lord God, lead me to Your rules. Teach me how You want me to live. Amen.

THE BIG TEN

"Teach them to do all the things I have told you."
MATTHEW 28:20

God wants you to show others through your good behavior how He wants His people to live, and He gave us ten special rules—the Ten Commandments—to help us:

1. Have no other god but the one and only God.
2. Don't worship statues or any other fake god.
3. Always use God's name with respect.
4. Remember Sunday as a holy day, a special day to honor God.
5. Respect your parents.
6. Don't kill.
7. If you marry someday, be true to the person you marry.
8. Don't steal.
9. Don't lie.
10. Don't be jealous.

Memorize them so you can live by them and share them with others.

Dear God, I promise to do my Best to honor You By oBeying Your commands. Amen.

GOD, I LOVE YOU

*Jesus said to him, "You must love the Lord
your God with all your heart and with all
your soul and with all your mind."*
MATTHEW 22:37

God made you so He could love you. He made you so He could love you not just when He created you, not just today or tomorrow—but forever! The Bible says, "God is love" (1 John 4:8), and that's why He sent Jesus to pay the price for your sins. God loves you so much He has a place waiting for you in heaven. He never, ever wants to be apart from you, not even when your life on earth is through.

One of God's rules is to love Him back. As you get to know Him better and discover how awesome He is, God will fill your heart to overflowing with His love. Then you will have plenty to give back to Him and to others. One way to show God you love Him is by telling Him so. You can also show Him by doing kind, loving things for others. What are some loving and kind things you've done today?

Dear God, I love You. Let Your love
grow big inside my heart. Amen.

LOVE ONE ANOTHER

"I give you a new Law. You are to love each other.
You must love each other as I have loved you."
JOHN 13:34

Jesus gave us an important law: love each other. Can you name a few people who love you?

How do you know you are loved? Maybe because they tell you so, keep you safe, or do nice things for you. We show love for each other in many different ways. You might not have thought of some of them.

The Bible says love is patient, love is kind, love doesn't get jealous. Love is humble—it thinks of others before itself. Love tries to do what's right, and it isn't selfish. Love doesn't get angry. It always forgives. Love hates what's bad, but it loves what's true. Love doesn't give up, not even when other people are hard to love. Love believes in and hopes for the best (1 Corinthians 13:4–8).

Are you surprised by the many ways we show love for each other?

Dear Jesus, teach me to love others By Being patient, kind, unselfish, and forgiving. Help me to love others the way you love me. Amen.

WAIT A SECOND!

*Always be humble and gentle. Patiently put
up with each other and love each other.*
EPHESIANS 4:2 CEV

God wants us to improve our patience—the ability to think about how others feel and not be selfish about what we want. Patience is one way to show others you love them. It can be one of the hardest ways to love, especially if someone gets in the way of something you want.

For example, imagine your mom promises to take you shopping for something special that you want to buy. . .but then she gets busy with work. Waiting patiently until she's ready might not be easy. But having patience is one way to show your mom you love her.

How good are you at patience? Is it one of your best behaviors or does it need some help? Think about it. Are you patient when others get to go first? Are you patient when you're busy and a younger sibling wants your attention? Impatience is easy. Patience takes practice. Work a little harder at patience this week.

Father, waiting is hard sometimes, and I
don't like waiting. Will you help me
to work on my patience? Amen.

KINDNESS COUNTS!

You must be kind to each other.
Think of the other person.
EPHESIANS 4:32

When God created your personality, He put a ton of room for kindness inside your heart. With God's guidance you can become a girl who notices when someone needs help. You could clear the table after dinner without being asked. You can be friendly and welcoming to kids who seem shy or lonely. You might share your things or give compliments that help others see the goodness in themselves. Or maybe you could clean up the mess your younger sister or brother made. You can also become a good listener and an encourager. God wants to help you be awesome when it comes to sharing your kindness!

Kindness is one way to show others you love them. It is also a way to show others you know Jesus and are trying to be kind like He is. When they see your good example, others might share their kindness too.

Dear God, thank You for showing me the many ways I can be kind and caring toward others. Thank You for growing kindness inside my heart. Amen.

29

MY HEART

*Keep your heart pure for out of it are
the important things of life.*
PROVERBS 4:23

The Bible has a lot to say about the heart.

You know that your heart is the main organ that keeps the blood and oxygen flowing throughout your body. If your heart stopped working, your body would die. But the Bible speaks about a different kind of heart. It is an invisible place God put deep inside you. It's where your personality is stored. This is the heart that makes you YOU.

All your thoughts and attitudes are stored there. It is your decision-making center. You can allow good things inside, or you can allow not-so-good things. Your conscience is in there too, reminding you that God wants you to do what is right and keep your heart pure. Our human hearts are sinful, but there's hope. God sent His perfect Son, Jesus, to take the punishment for our sins. If we are sorry for the wrong things we do, God will forgive us. He will make our hearts clean and pure again, and then it's our job to follow Jesus' good example.

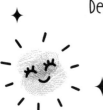

Dear God, forgive me for allowing sin into my heart. Please clean my heart and make it pure again. Amen.

GREEN-EYED MONSTER

*If you have jealousy in your heart and fight to
have many things, do not be proud of it.*
JAMES 3:14

Jealousy is feeling unhappy because someone else has
what you want.

Maybe you've heard of William Shakespeare. He wrote
a bunch of famous plays a long time ago. In one of his plays,
Shakespeare called jealousy a "green-eyed monster." Now
imagine the ugliest green-eyed monster ever. Draw it and
label it: JEALOUSY. Put your drawing in your room where
you can see it. Jealousy can make you feel angry, hurt, and
not good enough. Jealousy gets in the way of you loving
yourself, others, and even God. It's a sin you don't want
inside your heart.

Look at the picture you drew and say "No!" to jealousy.
Ask God to help you focus on being grateful for what you
have and trust Him to provide everything you need. And
try thinking about kids who have less than you. What you
already have could be what they want and wish for.

Lord God, when I feel jealous, help me to
focus more on You and what I have
instead of what I want. Amen.

31

WHAT IS HUMILITY?

In fact, everyone should be humble toward everyone else. The Scriptures say, "God opposes proud people, but he helps everyone who is humble."
1 PETER 5:5 CEV

God wants people with humility in their hearts. *Humility* means you don't think of yourself as better or more important than anyone else. It means focusing on others instead of yourself.

For example, if you receive an award or other honor, it's fine to be proud of your accomplishment. But humility is remembering you didn't do it alone. God and others helped you. You should acknowledge their help and thank them.

Humility is considering how others feel. Instead of saying, "Look what I did!" humility is telling others, "You did a great job!" Humility is saying, "I'm sorry" when you mess up. You show humility by being caring, understanding, and kind. God wants you to be a role model for humility. It's another way to show others you love them.

God, You made us to love and serve one another. Teach me to be humble by being sensitive to the way others feel. Help me to see everyone as my equal and to treat them that way. Amen.

MY BEST IS GOOD ENOUGH

Do your best to know that God is pleased with you.
Be as a workman who has nothing to be ashamed of.
2 TIMOTHY 2:15

God's directions in the Bible teach us the difference between right and wrong. God is pleased when we choose what's right. But sometimes we mess up. We choose wrong, and that leads to feelings of guilt.

Maybe you've felt that way. You wanted to do the right thing, but you messed up and now you feel guilty. You can turn that guilt around! You made a mistake, but that's okay. Mistakes are nothing to be ashamed of. Everyone makes them.

God allows mistakes so we learn to do better next time. All He asks is for you to do your best and remember you aren't perfectly perfect. Doing your best means trying even if you don't always succeed. As hard as you try, you will never choose the right way 100 percent of the time. Forgive yourself when you mess up and know that God forgives you too.

Dear heavenly Father, I try my best to do what's right. But sometimes I mess up. Thank You for loving and forgiving me anyway. Amen.

LOVE ISN'T SELFISH

Whenever people are jealous or selfish,
they cause trouble and do all sorts of cruel things.
JAMES 3:16 CEV

Is it selfish to make yourself a snack and leave the mess you made for someone else to clean up? Is it selfish to interrupt your mom when she's on the phone? Is it selfish at dinnertime to tell everyone about your day and not ask about theirs? When you don't get what you want, do you huff and puff and storm off to your room?

The Bible says love isn't selfish. It reminds us to think about how others feel. Selfishness can be sneaky. It is more complicated than refusing to share your things or wanting your way all the time. Noticing it takes practice. Selfishness can be disguised as complaining when you don't get what you want, pouting when you don't win a game, and thinking you are more important than others. God didn't put selfishness inside your heart. You don't want it there. Be on the lookout for it today.

Dear God, please help me to know when I'm being selfish. Remind me to be considerate of others and their feelings. Amen.

GET OVER IT

If you are angry, do not let it become sin.
Get over your anger before the day is finished.
EPHESIANS 4:26

She lost her temper, blew a fuse, hit the ceiling, and went through the roof! That's a funny way to imagine what anger looks like.

Some things in life make us feel angry, and sometimes for a good reason. But anger can lead us to revenge—wanting to get back at the person who made us angry—and that's not good. The Bible says to get over your anger quickly.

How can you do that? Don't allow anger to stay in your heart. Share how you feel. Talk about it with someone you trust. Especially, tell Jesus. Ask Him to help you get over your anger.

Think about a time you felt angry. What did you do with those angry feelings? Sometimes playing a sport or doing something fun is a good way to let go of anger. Can you think of other ways?

Dear Jesus, you know what happened, and you know why I'm angry. Will you help me let go of my angry feelings? I don't want them inside my heart. Amen.

I FORGIVE YOU

Then Peter came to Jesus and said,
"Lord, how many times may my brother sin against
me and I forgive him, up to seven times?"
MATTHEW 18:21

With God's help, we can be strong enough to forgive. Forgiveness is important. It is so important to God that He sent His Son, Jesus, to earth to forgive us for our sins so our hearts will be clean and pure enough for heaven someday.

Jesus' disciple Peter asked Him how many times he had to forgive someone. Peter thought seven times was fair. But Jesus answered, "Seventy times seven" (Matthew 18:21–22). Do the math. Did you answer 490 times? Jesus meant we should keep trying, again and again, to forgive others so we won't have unforgiveness inside our hearts.

Forgiveness can be hard sometimes, but God will give us the strength to do what He says is right. The Bible reminds us that love always forgives. When we learn to love others even when they behave badly, then it's easier to forgive. Is there someone you need to forgive today?

Dear Jesus, my friend hurt my feelings, and I don't feel much like forgiving her. Help me to remember that I love my friend, and love always forgives. Amen.

THAT'S GOOD!

Christian brothers, keep your minds thinking about whatever is true, whatever is respected, whatever is right, whatever is pure, whatever can be loved, and whatever is well thought of. If there is anything good and worth giving thanks for, think about these things.

PHILIPPIANS 4:8

God has filled up your heart with tons of good things that make you YOU. He's also given you eyes to see all the good things He made in the world and a brain to think about them.

Look around you. What do you see that's good? Now think about your family members. Name something good about each one. Think about your church or school. What's good about that? What's good about the world? What's good about today? What's good about God?

As you look for the good in people, places, and things, you will discover goodness all around you. God wants you to use your brain to think about the good things and guard your mind from thoughts that don't please Him. When you look for God's goodness in the world and others, you will find it. Ask God to grow more of His goodness in you!

Dear God, open my mind and my heart to everything good. Amen.

TRUE LOVE

"But love those who hate you. Do good to them.
Let them use your things and do not expect
something back. Your reward will be much.
You will be the children of the Most High."

LUKE 6:35

God made you to share all those things He says are good—things like kindness, patience, humility, forgiveness, and your readiness to let go of anger. Sharing God's goodness shows others you love them.

True love is sharing loving-kindness with others even when they don't deserve it. It is a kind of love that doesn't give up on others when they behave badly. True love reflects the way God loves us. God never gives up on us. He keeps loving us no matter what.

Do you think you can love others that way? What if someone hurt your feelings again and again? Could you still show them love by being patient and kind? When loving others is hard, you can always ask God to help you.

Dear God, help me to be more patient
and kind. I want to love others with a
true love like Yours. Amen.

THE GOLDEN RULE

"Do for other people what you would like to have them do for you."

LUKE 6:31

Gold is a precious metal. It has great value. Maybe you have a piece of gold jewelry. Maybe it's a special piece of jewelry, something you treasure. Jesus gave us an important rule to follow. It has more value than earthly gold. It's known as the Golden Rule, and if you remember, value, and treasure it, it will guide you to better relationships with family members, friends, teachers—everyone!

The rule says, "Do for other people what you would like to have them do for you." Would you like others to make fun of you, say unkind things about you, ignore you, or treat you badly? No! You'd want them to encourage you, say nice things about you, include you, and treat you kindly.

The next time someone gets on your nerves, hurts your feelings, or makes you angry, think about the Golden Rule. How will you treat them in return?

Dear Jesus, thank You for giving us the Golden Rule. It's one I will remember and do my best to obey. Amen.

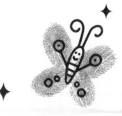

PEOPLE WITH A PURPOSE

Two are better than one, because they have good pay for their work. For if one of them falls, the other can help him up. But it is hard for the one who falls when there is no one to lift him up.
ECCLESIASTES 4:9–10

God didn't create you to wander through life alone. From the moment you were born, God put people around you to love you, care for you, and help you.

People will come into your life when you need them. Some will stay. Others will move on. But everyone who enters your life has a purpose. Some will teach you things about yourself you didn't know. Some will teach you how to use the skills and talents God gave you. Others will teach you about life and how to live it.

Throughout your life, you will make friends to have fun with. A few will become best friends, girls who love you just as you are and encourage you to be even better. Look for friends who know Jesus. Then you can help each other become more like Him.

Dear God, thank You for giving me people who will help and teach me. Amen.

FAMILIES

From now on you are not strangers and people who are not citizens. You are citizens together with those who belong to God. You belong in God's family.
EPHESIANS 2:19

Moms, dads, sisters, brothers, grandparents, aunts, uncles, cousins, stepparents, foster parents. . . God put you in a family with people who will care for you and love you.

Families come in all shapes and sizes. What does yours look like? You might think a family is made up only of people you are related to or live with. But the word *family* can have another meaning. It can mean a group of people who have something special in common. For example, you have a family of friends—the kids you hang out with. You also have a church family—those people you worship with every Sunday. The biggest family of all is God's family. It's a huge family made up of everyone who loves Jesus and accepts Him as their Savior. And God invites everyone to be part of it.

Father God, thank you for my family, the one I live with. Thank you for making me a part of other families too. Amen.

41

SAVIOR

We have seen and are able to say that the Father sent His Son to save the world from the punishment of sin.
1 JOHN 4:14

God wants you and everyone He's ever created to live with Him in heaven when their time on earth is done. To get to heaven, our hearts need to be clean of sin. But we all mess up and have sin-stained hearts—because apart from God, our hearts are very bad. But there's hope! God sent His Son, Jesus, to save us from that sin.

Jesus took all of our sin into His own heart, and He took the punishment we deserve so we won't have to. When we tell God we are sorry for our sin and ask Jesus to forgive us for the wrong we've done, we become members of God's family! Jesus will make a place for us in heaven, ready and waiting for us when we get there.

Another name for Jesus is *Savior* because He saves us from our sin. He makes us part of God's family forever. Thanks to Him, nothing can ever separate us from God.

Dear God, thank you for sending Jesus to get rid of our sin and make us ready for heaven. Amen.

MY FRIENDS AND ME

The sweet smell of incense can make you feel good, but true friendship is better still.
PROVERBS 27:9 CEV

God made you to have friends, and He made you to be a friend too. When God created you, He already knew who your friends would be. Not just the friends you have now, but those you will have all throughout your life.

Some friends will be with you only for a while. Others will stay. They will become your best friends, true friends. Think about it. What does it mean to be a true friend? Take a few minutes to make a list. Did you say things like being trustworthy, helpful, caring, forgiving, and kind? Those are just some of the qualities of a true friend.

True friends help each other become even better. They accept each other just as they are. They encourage and stick up for each other. They love each other even when loving is hard. Friendship isn't just having many friends, it's more about having good, true friends.

Thank you, God, for my friends, those I have now and the friends I'll meet later. Amen.

BE A CHAMPION!

So comfort each other and make each other strong as you are already doing.
1 THESSALONIANS 5:11

If you imagined yourself as a champion, what would you look like? Would you be smiling and holding a big trophy? When you think of the word *champion*, winning might first come to mind. But the word has another meaning: to stand up for a cause or someone who needs help.

What would you do if the kids at your lunch table made fun of a classmate? Would you speak up to defend your classmate or would you stay silent? God created you to be a champion for everything that is good and right. He wants you to encourage others and help them be strong so they always feel good about themselves.

Wouldn't you love to be a champion? Be the kind of girl who stands up for others and wants everyone to know they are important, valued, and loved.

Dear God, help me not to be shy about standing up for what's right. I want to be someone who helps others feel strong and good about themselves. Amen.

A LITTLE HELP, PLEASE

Help each other in troubles and problems.
This is the kind of law Christ asks us to obey.
GALATIANS 6:2

You can become the kind of girl who uses another of God's great qualities—helping. Jesus always has His eyes open for those in need and is ready and willing to help them. You can be like Jesus too.

Maybe you notice a friend having trouble with math, something you are good at. You offer to help with her math skills. Maybe you see your little brother is sad because no one will play with him. You stop what you're doing to play for a while. You can help in many different ways. Don't wait for someone to ask, just help—because that's what Jesus does for you. Each time you lend a hand, you are obeying Jesus' law to help others with their problems and troubles. And that is pleasing to God.

Father, I want to help others like Jesus says I should. Open my eyes to those who need help. Show me how to help them. Amen.

GOSSIP, SECRETS, AND RUMORS

*One who hurts people with bad talk
separates good friends.*
PROVERBS 16:28

The Bible's book of Proverbs was mainly written by King Solomon. He had asked God for wisdom, and God answered with a big "Yes!" Scripture calls Solomon the wisest man who ever lived, and the book of Proverbs is loaded with good advice that's helpful for getting along with others.

Proverbs 16:28 says, "Bad talk separates good friends." When we talk about others in a negative way, telling secrets and spreading gossip and rumors, it not only separates us from our friends, but it also separates us from God.

It hurts people when we say unkind things about them. It hurts God too. When He saved you, God put it in your heart to speak well of others and to build them up instead of cutting them down.

Dear God, when I get together with my friends, I sometimes forget to recognize "Bad talk." Thank You for reminding me to notice and not to say anything hurtful or unkind. Amen.

46

WISDOM

The fear of the Lord is the beginning of much learning. Fools hate wisdom and teaching.

PROVERBS 1:7

In Proverbs 1:7, Solomon talks about "the fear of the Lord." The word *fear* doesn't mean to be afraid as much as it does to honor God by respecting Him and His laws.

God is the source of all wisdom, and if you ask He will help you to know the difference between right and wrong (James 1:5). He wants you to trust that His way is the right way. Everyone struggles with that. We do what we want instead of what God wants. We mess up, we fail, and sometimes we get hurt. When that happens, God can give us wisdom to learn from our mistakes so we can do better next time.

Think about a time you messed up and did something you knew was wrong. What did you learn from your mistake? When King Solomon prayed and asked God for wisdom, God answered, "Yes!" You can pray the same way. Ask God to provide you with wisdom to know right from wrong. Then do what's right.

Dear God, give me wisdom to know right from wrong. I will honor you by doing what's right. Amen.

FRIENDS STICK TOGETHER

A man who has friends must be a friend, but there is a friend who stays nearer than a brother.
PROVERBS 18:24

Jesus is the best friend you will ever have. When things get difficult, you can always count on Him. He will stay with you no matter what! Jesus will love you, help you, and fight for you like He did for His disciples. When they were in trouble or had problems, Jesus didn't walk away and leave them alone. He stayed to help them through their difficult times.

God wants you to be a friend like Jesus is—reliable and trustworthy. Wouldn't you love to be the kind of friend who sticks by your friends to help when they need you? As you learn to help others through their difficult times, you will become an even better friend. Can you name a time you went through some trouble and a friend stayed to help? How did it make you feel?

Dear Jesus. I don't want to Be shy or afraid to stick By my friends when they have trouBle. Show me how to Be strong for them. Teach me how to help. Amen.

SWEET WORDS

Oil and perfume make the heart glad,
so are a man's words sweet to his friend.
PROVERBS 27:9

When He made you, God gave you ears to hear with. Spend time today listening to the things people say.

Sweet words—words that are kind, caring, and encouraging—are pleasing to God's ears. Sour words—words that are mean, hurtful, and discouraging—are not.

Words have power. Think about what they can do. Words can make others feel good about themselves, or words can cut them down. Be the kind of girl who uses her words wisely. Say things that are kind, supportive, and reassuring. If a friend is feeling not-so-good about herself, encourage her with loving, comforting, and uplifting words. Remind her that God loves her, and so do you. The words you choose can help your friend feel hopeful, confident, and strong.

When you use sweet words with others, you are setting an example for them to use sweet words too.

Dear God, please add more sweet words to my vocabulary. Teach me to use my words to encourage, comfort, and guide others to feel good about themselves. Amen.

SOUR WORDS

O Lord, put a watch over my mouth.
Keep watch over the door of my lips.
PSALM 141:3

When you listened closely with the ears God gave you, maybe you heard talk that wasn't so sweet, things like swear words, angry and mean words, lies, dirty jokes, discouraging words, and words that make fun of people. These are never pleasing to God.

Sour words are all around us. It's good that you notice! If you catch yourself saying something unkind or disrespectful, ask God to forgive you right away. Then do your best not to use that sort of language.

Maybe you heard people use God's and Jesus' names in ways that are disrespectful and rude. Think about the ten big rules God gave us, the Ten Commandments. The third rule says, "Always use God's name with respect." When speaking about God and Jesus, everyone should follow the rule. Be careful when choosing your words. They should show honor and respect to God, Jesus, and everyone else.

Lord God, please forgive me if disrespectful words slip from my mouth. I want my words to be pleasing to you and to others. Amen.

LISTEN!

*My Christian brothers, you know everyone
should listen much and speak little.
He should be slow to become angry.*
JAMES 1:19

God is the best listener. He is never too busy to listen to your prayers. And when God listens to you, He listens carefully giving you His undivided attention. He understands what you need.

Part of being a good friend is being a good listener. God gave you ears to hear with and a brain to think about what you hear. And He wants you to have patience. If a friend had a problem and told you about it, would you be a good listener? If you were busy, would you take time to listen carefully and care about her words? Good listeners listen! They listen and don't say much because they want to show others that their words are important.

Here's another question: Would you be a good listener if you and a friend disagreed over something? Good listening often helps calm angry feelings and leads to forgiveness.

God, sometimes I'm too quick to speak when instead I should be quiet and listen. Teach me to listen carefully, patiently, and with understanding. Amen.

51

FRIENDSHIP CHECKUP

Let us help each other to love others and to do good.
HEBREWS 10:24

Would you like to be more like Jesus by helping others love each other and do what's right? You can help by being a good friend, setting the best example, and by sharing what you know about Jesus and how He wants us to live. You've been learning about all the wonderful things that make you YOU. Now decide how to use them to help others become even better. Answer these questions:

- How might you help a friend who uses sour language or unkind words?
- How might you help a friend to overcome being jealous?
- How might you help a friend become more forgiving?
- What is the most important thing you would tell your friends about Jesus?

Maybe those were hard questions to answer. It can feel uncomfortable talking with your friends about Jesus and guiding them to become more like Him. Pray about it and ask Jesus to help you.

Lord Jesus, show me how to help others become more like You. Amen.

MOMS AND DADS

"Honor your father and your mother, as the Lord your God has told you. So your life may be long and it may go well with you in the land the Lord your God gives you."

DEUTERONOMY 5:16

Parents can be difficult to understand. They make rules you don't like, they tell you what to do, and they might even embarrass you in front of your friends. Even if your parents do things that you don't appreciate, God still wants you to honor them.

Honoring your parents means always treating them with respect. When God created you, He planned for your mom, dad, and other adults to help you grow up. He gave them wisdom to guide you.

Wisdom is something that increases with time. Your parents had experiences you will face in the future. Those experiences have taught them about keeping you safe, about helping you grow up with good values, and having confidence in who God made you to be. So trust and honor your mom or dad. They love you!

Dear God, please forgive me for those times I haven't honored my parents. Amen.

SISTERS AND BROTHERS

Keep on loving one another as brothers and sisters.
HEBREWS 13:1 NIV

Although God put sisters and brothers together in the same family, He made each one different and special. Sometimes siblings get jealous. They want something the other has or wish they were more like the other. Trouble between siblings can push aside all the good things God wants to grow inside our hearts.

The Bible tells us Jesus grew up with siblings. It doesn't explain much about their relationship, but we know Jesus had only good things in His heart. We can be sure He used all that goodness to live peacefully with his sisters and brothers.

Even if you don't have siblings at home, you do have brothers and sisters in Christ. You can get along better with them by behaving more like Jesus. Celebrate when good things happen for your sister or brother. And if you wish you were more like your sibling, remember that God made you YOU! You are awesome and special just as you are.

· ·

Dear Jesus, you know what it's like to have sisters and brothers. I love my siblings. Help us to always be patient, gentle, and kind toward each other. Amen.

DESCENDANTS AND ANCESTORS

[God] took [Abram] outside and said, "Now look up into the heavens and add up the stars, if you are able to number them." Then He said to him, "Your children and your children's children will be as many as the stars."
GENESIS 15:5

The Bible tells about Abram, who had no children. God told Abram to look at the stars and count them if he could. Then God made a promise to Abram: He said Abram would have children, and his children would have children, and their children would have children. . . . Abram would have more descendants—family that came after him—than he ever could count!

You have ancestors—family that came before you—more than you can count. When God created you, you were the next in a long line of family members. God gave you parents, grandparents, great-grandparents, great-great-grandparents and on and on. . . . Talk with your parents and grandparents about your ancestors. See how much they know about those who came before you. What might you have in common with your long-ago family?

Heavenly Father, thank you for my ancestors. I hope I meet them in heaven someday. Amen.

PROMISES, PROMISES. . .

God cannot lie. We who have turned to Him can have great comfort knowing that He will do what He has promised.
HEBREWS 6:18

God's promise to provide Abram with descendants is just one of many promises He made. The Bible is filled with God's promises not only to the people in the Bible but also to you!

God's Word holds His promises for all of us. You can count on God to follow through with His promises because it is impossible for Him to lie. God cannot lie because He is 100 percent good all the time. It's a sin to lie, and there is no sin in God. He has never sinned, and He never will because God is perfectly perfect.

The Bible says God promises never to leave you or let you be alone (Hebrews 13:5). He hears your voice and your prayers (Psalm 116:1). You can always count on God's words in the Bible to teach you and show you what to do (Psalm 119:105).

Dear God, You always tell me the truth. I know I can trust You to do exactly what You've promised. Amen.

GOD KNOWS WHAT I NEED

And my God will give you everything you need because of His great riches in Christ Jesus.
PHILIPPIANS 4:19

Imagine you are praying, and you ask God for three things you want. What would they be?

God promises to always hear your prayers and to answer them. God doesn't promise, though, to give you exactly what you ask for all the time. Instead, He will give you exactly what you need. God knows better than you what you need and when you need it. The things you ask for might not be in His plan for you.

The Bible says God knew you before He put you together, and He wrote down all the days of your life before any of them came to be (Psalm 139:16). God knows what you need every day. You can trust Him to provide it. That doesn't mean you shouldn't ask God for what you want. Trust that He hears you. Then wait patiently, believing He will answer you in His own way and time.

Dear God, even when I don't get what I want, help me to trust in Your promise to provide whatever I need. Amen.

YES, NO, LATER

The Lord is good to those who wait for
Him, to the one who looks for Him.
LAMENTATIONS 3:25

What if nothing happened when you asked God for something you really, *really* wanted? Would you be angry with God? Would you give up asking?

God promises, "Call to Me, and I will answer you. And I will show you great and wonderful things which you do not know" (Jeremiah 33:3). Hang on to the last part of that promise. You can't know how God will answer your prayers. Sometimes He says yes right away, and sometimes, He says later. If God says no to you today, He might have something even better waiting for you.

The Bible says to be strong and wait for God (Psalm 27:14). It says God promises to be good to those who wait for Him and look for Him. So don't stop praying! Look to God and ask Him to reveal what He wants for you. Then be strong and wait. God made you, He loves you, and He will be good to you.

Father, when I ask You for something,
please help me to wait patiently
for You to answer. Amen.

WHEN I DON'T UNDERSTAND

Trust in the Lord with all your heart, and do not trust in your own understanding. Agree with Him in all your ways, and He will make your paths straight.
PROVERBS 3:5–6

Imagine you prayed patiently for what you wanted, and you were sure God would say yes. What you asked for was a good thing. But God said no. You wondered, *Why, God? Why didn't You give me what I asked for?*

One of the mysteries about God is that He sometimes does things we don't understand or like. His way of thinking is so much greater than ours, and what we think is best might not fit with His plan. One of the most difficult things is to keep trusting God when you don't understand Him.

But God promises if you agree that He knows best, He will keep you on the right path in life. He will lead where He wants you to go.

Oh, God, I don't understand why You said no to me. But please help me to accept Your answer. You made me. I trust that You love me and have good things planned for me. Amen.

59

WHEN I AM SAD

*He heals those who have a broken
heart. He heals their sorrows.*

PSALM 147:3

Have you ever been so sad it felt like a deep hurt inside your heart? When God created you, He knew you would feel many different emotions. Sadness would be one of them. Everyone is sad sometimes. Sadness can make you feel alone. It can make you feel like no one understands you—but God does! You can trust Him to help you through your sadness and heal your broken heart.

When God made you, He promised never to leave you. It's important to remember He is with you when you feel sad. You can talk with God about your sadness and ask Him to comfort you. Feeling sad can last a little while or much longer, and sometimes other emotions get mixed in. God gave you people you can trust to love and help you. Talk with them. Tell them how you feel, and don't be afraid to ask for help.

. . . .

Dear God, when I am sad, I will trust You to heal my sadness. Remind me I'm not alone. Lead me to those who can help. Amen.

TEARS IN A BOTTLE

You have seen how many places I have gone.
Put my tears in Your bottle. Are they not in Your book?
PSALM 56:8

In Psalm 56, David, the future king of Israel, is speaking to God. David is facing a ton of trouble. Through it all He prays, trusting God to be on his side. David says, "They are always thinking of ways to hurt me. They change my words to say what I didn't say. But, God, I will trust in You."

We can imagine David crying when he says, "Put my tears in Your bottle. Are they not in Your book?" David trusted God's promise to see his troubles and count every tear. He imagined God saving his tears in a bottle and listing each one in a book.

God will never forget the times you feel sad. He knows you so well! He remembers every situation that made you cry, and He keeps a record of each tear. God wants to wipe away your tears and see you happy again.

Father God, You know when I cry.
You count each tear and save it. Thank You
for caring and loving me so much. Amen.

GOD COMFORTS ME

We give thanks to the God and Father of our Lord Jesus Christ. He is our Father Who shows us loving-kindness and our God Who gives us comfort.

2 CORINTHIANS 1:3

When you feel sad or upset, what brings you comfort? Maybe you said a hug, or maybe some kind, loving words. God promises to comfort you with His loving-kindness.

Sometimes you are comforted just by knowing God is with you. His comfort comes through reading the Bible too, and by remembering that God loves you. Sometimes God will use other people to comfort you. Think of a time someone helped you when you felt sad or upset. What did that person say or do that helped? Now decide what you could do to help someone who is upset or sad.

The Bible says that God is close to the brokenhearted (Psalm 34:18). God's Spirit lives inside your heart. He is always nearby, ready to comfort you and show you how to provide comfort to others.

Dear God, your loving-kindness brings me comfort and peace. Teach me to be a comforter. Guide me to help others when they feel sad, upset, or alone. Amen.

JOY!

You will show me the way of life. Being with You is to be full of joy. In Your right hand there is happiness forever.
PSALM 16:11

When God saved you, He put joy in your heart. He promised you enough joy to last forever.

Joy and happiness are different. Happiness is a feeling you have when you do something fun, receive a gift you want, or reach a goal. Joy is an attitude you choose. If you planned an outside party for your birthday and it rained, you wouldn't be happy. But you could choose joy by concentrating on good things like spending time with your friends and getting plenty of attention on your special day.

Finding joy is connected to your relationship with Jesus. You can find joy knowing that He loves you and is always with you. When you put your trust in Jesus, He can turn your unhappiness to joy. He can show you how to have a positive attitude so you can find something good even on bad days.

. . . .

Dear Jesus, open my heart to the joy that's inside. Teach me to see all the good that's around me. Amen.

63

WHEN I FEEL AFRAID

*"Do not fear, for I am with you. Do not be afraid,
for I am your God. I will give you strength,
and for sure I will help you. Yes, I will hold you up
with My right hand that is right and good."*

ISAIAH 41:10

Everyone is afraid of something. Spiders, heights, the dark, speaking in front of a group, snakes, and storms—all are just a few common fears people have. There are other, more unusual, fears too, like hippopotomonstrosesquippedalio-phobia. (Think you can say it?) It's a real thing—the fear of long words. Or arachibutyrophobia, the fear of peanut butter sticking to the roof of your mouth!

Whatever makes you afraid, God promises to help you and give you strength to conquer your fear. Remember, you are His child. You don't need to be anxious about anything, because your heavenly Father is with you. He has everything under control.

It's okay to feel afraid. But when that feeling bubbles up inside you, talk with God and know He is there.

Dear God, when I feel afraid, I will remember You are with me, helping and protecting me. Amen.

GOD GIVES ME COURAGE

"Do not remember the things that have happened before. Do not think about the things of the past. See, I will do a new thing. It will begin happening now. Will you not know about it? I will even make a road in the wilderness, and rivers in the desert."
ISAIAH 43:18–19

If something unpleasant happened in the past, do you worry it might happen again? God has a promise for you. He says not to dwell on what happened, because He is doing something new. He will make a way for you to keep going without being afraid.

Would you like God to make you strong? That doesn't mean you will perform incredible feats of physical strength. But He can strengthen your character, courage, and will-ingness to keep moving forward even when you don't want to. Instead of worrying that some past event will happen again, ask God to give you courage to conquer your fear. Trust Him and see where He leads you.

Dear God, help me not to worry that something in the past will happen again. Help me to Be Brave and to keep moving forward. Amen.

ALONE

*"I will not leave you without help as children
without parents. I will come to you."*
JOHN 14:18

All girls and boys face situations when Mom or Dad can't be there. It can feel lonely, even scary the first time you go to sleepover camp, or when you start a new school, or when your parents trust you to stay home alone. When you feel lonely, remember you have a helper.

Jesus has promised, "I will not leave you without help as children without parents. I will come to you." You can trust the one who made you to always be with you. He is everywhere all the time, so you never have to worry He isn't in that new place or situation. God the Father says, "I am the Lord your God Who holds your right hand, and Who says to you, 'Do not be afraid. I will help you' " (Isaiah 41:13).

Whenever you feel lonely, imagine Him taking your hand and guiding you through that new situation. He is your helper. He will never leave you.

Lord God, I feel afraid to do this By myself.
Take my hand. Let's do it together. Amen.

GOD GIVES ME CONFIDENCE

*So do not throw away your confidence;
it will be richly rewarded.*
HEBREWS 10:35 NIV

God knew you would need perseverance and faith to face hard times and challenges. So God promises His children that they can have the confidence to come to Him for help. "Let us then approach God's throne of grace with confidence, so that we may receive mercy and find grace to help us in our time of need" (Hebrews 4:16).

It takes confidence in God to face a new or scary situation. But God keeps His promises and will reward your confidence (Hebrews 10:36). Each time you attempt something difficult, whether you are successful or not, you can learn and grow closer to God.

When you succeed, your reward is discovering God can do things through you that you never thought were possible. When you fail, you build your faith by reading about God's promises in the Bible and doing what the Bible says (James 1:22–25). Either way, when you face a challenge and find yourself thinking *I can't*—stop. Think. Say, "God can!" and ask Him for help.

- -

Dear God, thank you for reminding me
that I can have confidence in you. Amen.

GOD IS MY SAFE PLACE

He will cover you with His wings. And under
His wings you will be safe. He is faithful like
a safe-covering and a strong wall.

PSALM 91:4

When a mother hen senses danger, she covers her chicks with her wings. The babies feel safe there because their mother is strong and faithful. They trust her to protect them.

God is like a mother hen. When you trust Him for protection, He promises to be your safe place. Psalm 91 says God will keep you from being afraid of trouble. He will tell His angels to surround you and care for you. When you were little and something frightened you at night, maybe you jumped into bed with your parents and pulled the covers over your head. You felt safe there lying near Mom or Dad.

It's like that with God. You can imagine Him covering you in a blanket of peace, keeping you safe from what's happening around you. God is your safe place in all kinds of trouble. He loves and cares for you.

Dear God, when trouBle comes, You are my
safe place and my protector. I trust You,
and I will not Be afraid. Amen.

68

JESUS IS MY RESTING PLACE

"Come to Me, all of you who work and have heavy loads. I will give you rest."
MATTHEW 11:28

Homework, music practice, dance lessons, sports, other after-school activities, plans with friends, chores at home, family commitments—it's all so overwhelming! It's too much!

When you feel maxed out, Jesus has a promise for you. He says, "Come to me. I will give you rest." God didn't create you to be so overscheduled you feel swamped, tired, and upset. Give that stress to Jesus. Let Him handle the stuff that's weighing you down. Sometimes, you just need to go someplace quiet where you can talk with Jesus and say, "Please take my worries and concerns. Hold on to them while I take a break and calm myself down."

You can count on Jesus to handle everything that's stressing you out. To get a good rest, you might need to give up a few things you don't need to do. Ask Jesus to help you decide.

. . . .

Dear Jesus, it's all too much. I need a break. Please take my worries and my stress. Show me what to do so I can get some rest. Amen.

SWEET SLEEP

You will not be afraid when you lie down.
When you lie down, your sleep will be sweet.
PROVERBS 3:24

Do you sometimes lie in bed at night unable to sleep? Maybe you and your best friend argued today, and her words are playing over and over in your head. Maybe you're worried about a math test tomorrow. Whatever it is that keeps you awake, God promises you sweet sleep. He wants to bless you with a good night's rest.

Do you remember Isaiah 43:18? It's a Bible verse to memorize. God says, "Do not remember the things that have happened before. Do not think about the things of the past." Let go of what happened today. Let go of thoughts about tomorrow too because Jesus says, "Do not worry about tomorrow. Tomorrow will have its own worries. The troubles we have in a day are enough" (Matthew 6:34).

When you lie down tonight, say your prayers. Then tell God goodnight and go to sleep.

Father, when I lie down, help me not to think about today or worry about tomorrow. Bless me with sweet, restful sleep. Amen.

A PSALM TO REMEMBER

The Lord is my Shepherd. I will have everything I need.
PSALM 23:1

God put a wonderful psalm in the Bible to remind you that Jesus is like a good shepherd watching over his sheep. Memorize Psalm 23. Whenever you need to feel nearer to Him, you can say it as your prayer:

The Lord is my Shepherd. I will have everything I need. He lets me rest in fields of green grass. He leads me beside the quiet waters. He makes me strong again. He leads me in the way of living right with Himself which brings honor to His name. Yes, even if I walk through the valley of the shadow of death, I will not be afraid of anything, because You are with me. You have a walking stick with which to guide and one with which to help. These comfort me. You are making a table of food ready for me in front of those who hate me. You have poured oil on my head. I have everything I need. For sure, You will give me goodness and loving-kindness all the days of my life. Then I will live with You in Your house forever. Amen.

FOREVER

Yes, even if I walk through the valley of the shadow of death, I will not be afraid of anything, because You are with me.

PSALM 23:4

When God made your body, He didn't plan for it to last forever. God knew we needed bodies to live here on earth. When our time here is done, our bodies will die. If we've put our trust in Jesus, God promises us new, perfect bodies in our forever home.

Thinking about death can be scary because so much is unknown. God says we shouldn't be afraid of dying. When your earthly body dies, the part that makes you YOU will live on forever.

Maybe you know someone who passed away. When a loved one dies, we feel sad. God promises to comfort us in our sadness. There is no sadness in heaven, so you can imagine the person happy there, living with God, ready to see you again one day.

Dear God, if I worry about myself or a loved one dying, You will comfort me and help me not to be afraid. Death isn't the end of everything. It is the beginning of a new life in heaven with You. Amen.

JESUS GUIDES AND HELPS ME

You have a walking stick with which to guide and one with which to help. These comfort me.
PSALM 23:4

Psalm 23 speaks about Jesus having a walking stick to guide and help us. In ancient times shepherds used sticks to scare off predators. And if a lamb strayed from the flock, the shepherd used his stick to gently guide it back.

God has always wanted Jesus to guide you through life. You can count on Jesus to fight your enemies. If you mess up and don't follow where He's leading, He will gently nudge you back. God adds His protection too. He says, "Do not be afraid. . . . I have called you by name. You are Mine! When you pass through the waters, I will be with you. When you pass through the rivers, they will not flow over you. . . . For I am the Lord your God. . . . You are of great worth in My eyes. . . . I love you" (Isaiah 43:1–4).

Dear God, thank you for protecting me and for sending Jesus as my helper and guide. Amen.

I AM HONORED AND LOVED

You are making a table of food ready for me in front of those who hate me. You have poured oil on my head. I have everything I need.
PSALM 23:5

Hopefully you don't have enemies who hate you. But you might not consider some people as friends because they are mean to you or unkind. Psalm 23 speaks about that too.

When someone is unkind toward you, you can imagine Jesus setting up a special banquet table for you while that person looks on. Jesus welcomes you to His table. He even pours a little oil on your head. Why would He do that? In ancient times, the host would pour a little perfumed oil on the head of his guest. It was a way of saying, "I honor your presence here." God created you to have friends who honor you. When people are unkind, remember Jesus is your friend. He shows you respect and welcomes you as His honored guest.

- -

Dear Jesus, when others are against me, you make me feel special and dearly loved. Thank you for being my friend. Amen.

TEMPTATION

*But the Lord is faithful. He will give you
strength and keep you safe from the devil.*
2 THESSALONIANS 3:3

You do have an enemy. We all do. He's the devil, and he is real. The devil is God's archenemy. He is at work on earth, trying to undo all the good things God does.

When God made you, He knew you would need strength to stand up to the devil and say no to him when he tempts you. Temptation is something you need to watch out for. The devil will try to trick you by encouraging you to do something wrong. He even tempted Jesus to sin. But Jesus said, "No!"

Jesus has this promise for you: When you put your faith in Him, He will keep you safe from the devil. He will make you strong enough to recognize the devil's tricks and say no to them. Can you think of a time the devil tempted you to do something wrong? Did you give in to his temptation?

Dear Jesus, give me wisdom to recognize the devil's tricks. Give me strength to resist and to do what is right. Amen.

GOD FORGIVES ME

*If we tell Him our sins, He is faithful and we
can depend on Him to forgive us of our sins.
He will make our lives clean from all sin.*

1 JOHN 1:9

Imagine you totally messed up, and you feel ashamed.
You've told no one what you did. Still, the big mess-up is
always on your mind. You feel guilty, and you wish it had
never happened.

Would you tell God about it, or would you keep it to
yourself? God already knows. He sees and knows everything
and doesn't want you dragging all that guilt and shame
around. He has this promise for you: if you tell Him what
you did and ask Him to forgive you, He will. God will clean
your heart of that sin as if it never happened.

When He made you, God wanted you to learn from your
mess-ups, not to repeat them again and again. Remember,
God is on your side. You can tell Him when you mess up,
and He will always love and forgive you.

Dear God, I've messed up and I'm
ashamed. I'm sorry for what I did.
Please forgive me. Amen.

IT'S ALL GOOD

We know that God makes all things work together for the good of those who love Him and are chosen to be a part of His plan.
ROMANS 8:28

You can trust God to blend the positive and negative experiences in your life into something good. God's plan for you is to become more like Jesus. Jesus is the perfect example of what God wants everyone to be—kind, caring, loving, forgiving, wise, patient, gentle, faithful, fair—Jesus is everything good!

God promises to weave together all the parts of your life to make you more like His Son. God will teach you and guide you. Some of what you learn won't be easy. It will come as a result of you (or even someone else) messing up and maybe messing up big. But in that mess there will be a lesson. If you remember the lessons and put to use what you learn, you will grow to be more caring, loving, forgiving, and kind.

Have you ever trusted God during a hard time in your life? What happened?

Dear God, thank You for working everything together in my life to make me more like Jesus. Amen.

SUPERGLUE

Who can keep us away from the love of Christ?
Can trouble or problems? Can suffering wrong
from others or having no food? Can it be because
of no clothes or because of danger or war?
ROMANS 8:35

If you want something to stick really well, you use the best glue. If you use a superglue, you have faith it will never let go.

Faith is like the superglue that bonds Jesus' love to your heart. It is the most important part of your relationship with Him. When you put your faith in Jesus, His love will help you through every kind of trouble or problem. If someone is mean to you or hurts you, Jesus' love will protect and comfort you. If a homework assignment makes you feel like giving up, Jesus' love will keep you going. Wherever you are and whatever you need, Jesus is there loving you, helping you, and making you strong.

Jesus has power over everything, and you have His promise that nothing will ever separate you from His love.

Dear Jesus, when my world is coming apart,
you hold me together and your love
gives me strength. Amen.

PROMISE KEEPER

"Know then that the Lord your God is God, the faithful God. He keeps His promise and shows His loving-kindness to those who love Him and keep His Laws, even to a thousand family groups in the future."

DEUTERONOMY 7:9

When God made you, He promised to be with you all the days of your life. He promised if you love and follow Jesus, you will live forever in heaven someday. God is faithful to keep every one of His promises.

Think about the promises you make. Do you keep every one? If others see you are a promise keeper, they will know they can trust you. When you make a promise, don't ever say things like "I swear I will do it." Jesus says in Matthew 5:37, "Let your yes be YES. Let your no be NO. Anything more than this comes from the devil." Keep your promises simple. If you say that you will or won't do something, be true to your word. This will be pleasing to God.

Dear God, You are faithful to keep every promise. Help me to be wise about making promises. Keep me true to my word. Amen.

NONSENSE OR GOOD SENSE?

Your hands made me and put me together.
Give me understanding to learn Your Law.
PSALM 119:73

Pop quiz part one: Define *nonsense* and give an example.

Did you say nonsense is something foolish? What if you thought you could fly and jumped off a roof to prove it? That would be foolish (and dangerous too). It's nonsense to think people can fly.

God created you to have good sense. That means knowing the difference between what's right and wrong, or what's wise and foolish. Sometimes you might not be sure if something is right or wise. If you are unsure, instead of leaping into what you think is right, spend time praying to God. Ask Him to help you understand what He wants you to do. God will always lead you toward what's right.

Pop quiz part two: You are at a friend's house playing a video game when someone you don't know sends an instant message wanting to be your friend. What would be a good-sense response?

Heavenly Father, when I'm unsure about things, help me to make good-sense decisions. Guide me to what You want me to think and do. Amen.

A DIVIDED HEART

*Teach me your way, LORD, that I may rely
on your faithfulness; give me an undivided
heart, that I may fear your name.*

PSALM 86:11 NIV

When God made your heart, the part that holds your personality and makes you YOU, He gave you the responsibility of guarding what's in there. It's your job to decide what to allow and what to reject.

If you choose sin—things that displease God—it's like building a stone wall inside your heart that separates you from God. A divided heart cares more about pleasing you than pleasing God. A divided heart doesn't care or feel guilty about choosing sin.

Get in the habit of talking with God throughout the day and do your best to make good-sense decisions. God will help you guard your heart. If you aren't sure if something is right, He will teach you. We are all born with sinful hearts, but if you ask for God's forgiveness, He will create in you a clean heart through Jesus. He promises, "I will take away your heart of stone" (Ezekiel 36:26).

Lord God, please give me an undivided heart. I don't want anything to put a wall between me and you. Amen.

"*SHE* MADE ME DO IT!"

And so, dear friends, now that you know this, watch so you will not be led away by the mistakes of these sinful people. Do not be moved by them.

2 PETER 3:17

Imagine this: your parents have allowed you to use the Internet only with their supervision. They've blocked some sites because they don't want you there. A friend comes over. She has a phone with an app for one of those sites. The two of you are in your room watching videos your parents don't allow, and your mom walks in. You try to defend yourself. "*She* made me do it!"

Part of guarding your heart is not following the wrong decisions friends make. When friends lead you toward doing what's wrong, God allows you to decide yes or no. Have you ever been pressured by a friend to do something you didn't want to do? Was it hard to say no? The Bible says to watch what you do. Don't allow others to lead you away from God.

Dear God, it's hard sometimes to say no to my friends. Please give me strength to do what is right. Amen.

WHAT'S ON YOUR MIND?

*Do not act like the sinful people of the world.
Let God change your life. First of all, let Him
give you a new mind. Then you will know what
God wants you to do. And the things you do
will be good and pleasing and perfect.*
ROMANS 12:2

It isn't just people who can lead you from God. What you see and hear can too. God gave you a brain so you can think about what you see and hear.

Maybe you saw some kids playing with matches. You thought it looked like fun and wanted to try. Or maybe you heard a song with swear words or other not-so-nice lyrics, but you thought the music was cool so you wanted to hear it again. When your thoughts lead you toward doing what's wrong, ask God to give you a new mind.

The world is filled with sights and sounds designed to lead you away from Him. Keep your eyes and ears open. Choose what God wants you to do.

Dear God, when my thoughts lead me away
from You, give me a new mind. Help me
to obey and follow You. Amen.

83

WORDS OF WISDOM

A nation falls where there is no wise leading, but it is safe where there are many wise men who know what to do.

PROVERBS 11:14

When God created you, He gave you the ability to become wise. He didn't pour wisdom into your heart all at once. Instead, He helps you grow in wisdom as you learn to make good choices.

Sometimes you won't know what to do. You might weigh the pros and cons—the good things and bad things about a choice—and still not know. You could pray and not be sure about what God wants you to do. When that happens, ask God to give you wisdom and to lead you to people who can help you decide (James 1:5).

It's good to seek wisdom by talking things over with other Christians—people who know and love Jesus. If you had a tough choice to make right now, could you name three people you would go to for help? Why would you choose those three?

Dear God. I've thought about my choices. I've prayed. and still I can't decide. Please give me wisdom and lead me to Christian friends who can help. Amen.

84

DISCERNMENT DETECTIVE

*Teach me knowledge and good judgment,
for I trust your commands.*
PSALM 119:66 NIV

Some advice won't be wise. You can make a poor choice if you follow advice that doesn't agree with God's idea of right and wrong. God created you with the ability to use good sense and good judgment. He made you to be like a detective who "discerns"—identifies—whether the advice you receive agrees with the Bible and leads you toward Him.

Good advice never disagrees with what God says. You will recognize good advice by knowing what's in the Bible and remembering God's rules about how people should behave. Good advice will always lead you nearer to God and toward doing what you imagine Jesus would do.

Studying Jesus' story in the Bible—as found in Matthew, Mark, Luke, and John—can help with that. Talk with God about the advice you receive. Ask Him to give you good discernment about whether it's advice you should follow.

Father God, please bless me with discernment. Help me to recognize whether advice is good or bad. Show me what you want me to do. Amen.

BUT I WANT TO!

*Good judgment wins favor, but the way of
the unfaithful leads to their destruction.*
PROVERBS 13:15 NIV

God expects everyone to be faithful to Him and do what's right. But He gives us freedom to choose. He allows us to decide whether to obey Him. Sometimes we are faced with a choice where the wrong way looks more attractive. The devil loves leading us away from what's good.

Imagine you have a ton of homework to do when a friend invites you to go to the movies with her and her parents. Would you tell your mom you've finished your homework so you could go with your friend, or would you tell your friend you need to stay home and get your work done?

You might really, *really* want to go to the movies. But lying to your mom would be wrong, and making that wrong choice could lead to a punishment. Good judgment and choosing what's right is always pleasing to God—and your parents too!

Thank You, God, for giving me freedom to make my own decisions. If the wrong way looks good to me, help me to choose what's right. Amen.

FLIP A COIN

Man decides by throwing an object into the lap, but it is the Lord only who decides.
PROVERBS 16:33

God wants you to be wise about the devil's tricks, like when he's messing with your decision-making skills. The devil might tempt you with foolish tricks when you need to make a choice. Things like flipping a coin, drawing straws, saying a silly rhyme, and other random decision-making methods are fun when they're part of a game, but you should never use them as a way to decide something important.

When you put your faith in an object to help you decide, it dishonors God. It gives power to that object that rightfully belongs to Him. When you flip a coin, roll dice, or draw straws, you are relying on good luck instead of on God. Unless it is part of a game, use good sense instead of nonsense. Always trust God to be your decision maker. His are the only decisions that are good, right, and true.

Dear God. I won't rely on silly games to help with important decisions. I will trust You to guide me in the way I should go. Amen.

REMEMBER HIS WORDS

But as for you, hold on to what you have learned and know to be true. Remember where you learned them.
2 TIMOTHY 3:14

God will use the Bible to teach you His ways. Reading your Bible is another way you communicate with God. When you read its words, it's like God is speaking to you. Some of what you read will make you think about what's happening in your life right now. God wants you to remember what you read and store it in your heart. It's important to memorize Bible verses and think of them often. Here are three you can memorize today:

- "For God so loved the world that He gave His only Son. Whoever puts his trust in God's Son will not be lost but will have life that lasts forever" (John 3:16).
- "Do for other people what you would like to have them do for you" (Luke 6:31).
- "Give thanks to the Lord for He is good! His loving-kindness lasts forever!" (Psalm 107:1).

That's a great start! Make it a goal to memorize one verse each day.

Dear God, I will remember Your words and store them inside my heart. Amen.

I CHANGED MY MIND

Yes, I changed my mind. Does that show that I change my mind a lot? Do I plan things as people of the world who say yes when they mean no? You know I am not like that!
2 CORINTHIANS 1:17

You made a decision, but then you discovered it wasn't the best or right choice. You wondered, *Is it okay to change my mind?*

Rethinking a choice is using good sense. If you've chosen wrong, God allows do-overs. You never have to be shy about saying, "You know what? I'm not sure that was the right thing to do." If you make a wrong choice, God will lead you in the right direction. He will get you back on the path to follow Him.

Can you think of a time you made an important decision and then changed your mind? What happened? Learning from a wrong choice can help you make the right choice in the future. It can give you wisdom and lead you to help others if you see them making the same mistake.

Heavenly Father, thank You for helping me change my wrong choice to the right one. Amen.

THE WISE AND FOOLISH BUILDERS

*Do not be foolish. Understand what
the Lord wants you to do.*
EPHESIANS 5:17

When you read about Jesus in your Bible, you will find Him telling stories called *parables.* Jesus tells these stories to make you think. In the following story, He reminds you to make wise decisions:

"Whoever hears these words of Mine and does them, will be like a wise man who built his house on rock. The rain came down. The water came up. The wind blew and hit the house. The house did not fall because it was built on rock. Whoever hears these words of Mine and does not do them, will be like a foolish man who built his house on sand. The rain came down. The water came up. The wind blew and hit the house. The house fell and broke apart" (Matthew 7:24–27).

Disobeying Jesus and God leads to making poor decisions, and poor decisions often lead to bad endings.

Dear Jesus. I will read my Bible and learn from Your words. Amen.

HOW I SEE MYSELF

I praise you because of the wonderful way you created me. Everything you do is marvelous! Of this I have no doubt.
PSALM 139:14 CEV

Look in a mirror. Starting at the top of your head, describe what you look like: hair, eyes, nose, mouth, ears, skin. . .all the way down to your toes. God made your body. When He looks at you, God sees the beautiful girl He created. He wants you to see that girl too.

Maybe you wish your hair wasn't curly or your eyes were brown instead of green. God loves that curly hair and those green eyes. He designed them when He created you. Maybe you wish you were taller or thinner, shorter or heavier. God made you just as you are. He gave you a unique one-of-a kind body, and He wants you to love your body the way He does.

Now, look at yourself in the mirror again. List the wonderful things you see.

Dear God, help me to see my Body the way You do. I praise You for the wonderful way You created me. Thank You for making me ME! Amen.

HOW I SEE OTHERS

God does not show favor to one
man more than to another.
ROMANS 2:11

When you look at others, what's the first thing you see? Do you notice what they look like, their hair, eyes, nose, mouth, ears, skin. . .all the way down to their toes? Do you notice if they're taller or thinner, shorter or heavier? Here's another question, and one you should really think about: Do you *judge* others by how they look?

God made their bodies. He made them beautiful, just like He made yours, and that's how He wants you to see them. God made us all. He wants us to see each other as He does and to be respectful of these bodies He's made. When you look at the people around you, notice all the beautiful hair, eye, and skin colors. Celebrate tall, thin, short, heavy, and all the other ways God made us unique, different, and yet equal—no one better than the other. Each of us is one of God's amazing creations.

Dear God, help me to notice how everyone is beautiful on the outside. Open my eyes to the wonderful ways we are different and unique. Amen.

SELF-CONFIDENCE

I ask each one of you not to think more of himself than he should think. Instead, think in the right way toward yourself by the faith God has given you.
ROMANS 12:3

God made you to love who you are. He wants you to have confidence in yourself so you can be strong, make wise choices, and accomplish great things. Self-confidence is important. But it's more important to remember who gives you your confidence.

God is the one who makes you creative, talented, smart, strong, courageous, a leader, a problem solver. . . When you give more credit to yourself than you do God for your wonderfulness, then you might think you are better than everyone else—and that's never good.

You should love yourself because God made you and gave you all the great qualities that make you YOU. Thank Him today for loving you and for helping you to love yourself.

Father, I love who I am! I love that You made me with so many wonderful qualities. You made me in Your image, and I reflect who You are. Help me never to forget that. Amen.

ABLE

*God is able to do much more than we ask or
think through His power working in us.*
EPHESIANS 3:20

God made you able to do much more than you think.

There's an old story about a train that couldn't get over a mountain. It needed a strong engine to help. A little engine came along, maybe too small to help. "I think I can. I think I can," she said, trying to pull the heavy train. It wasn't easy. She tugged and she pulled. Then slowly, very slowly, the train started moving up, up. . .and finally over the mountaintop it went. "I thought I could! I thought I could!" the little engine said merrily as she chugged down the mountainside.

This story is a reminder that you are never too young or too small to accomplish great things. Your power comes from God working through you. With His help, and you giving it your all, you are able to change "I think I can" to "I know I can!"

. . . .

Dear God, with Your help, I know I can accomplish
much more than I thought I ever could. Amen.

LOOK CLOSER

When I saw it, I thought about it.
I looked and received teaching.
PROVERBS 24:32

God can help you to be an observer—to notice what's going on in His world and learn from it. There are many good things to notice, people having fun, being kind, and helping each other. You will notice bad things too, and people who are mean, unkind, and hurt each other.

Proverbs 24:32 reminds you to think about what you notice. What can you learn from what you see? Maybe you're unsure of some things happening in the world. You don't know if they are right or wrong, good or bad. Talk with God about it. Measure what you see against what God says in the Bible. Talk with Christian friends and family members too. See what they think.

A good observer examines everything carefully. Being a good observer helps you pick up signs about how other people feel. It's an important step toward understanding and helping others.

Dear God, open my eyes and ears to the world around me. Help me to learn from what I observe. Lead me to use what I learn to help others. Amen.

95

LEARN COMPASSION

Finally, all of you, be like-minded, be sympathetic, love one another, be compassionate and humble.
1 PETER 3:8 NIV

God desires that His followers be *compassionate*. It means you understand someone's suffering and you want to do something to help.

For example, a friend has trouble at home. You get how she feels because you've been through something similar. You can sympathize with the way she feels because you've felt that way too. You could think about what you needed when you had your trouble and use that to help your friend. Maybe she needs a hug and someone to talk to and pray with. She might need suggestions to point her in the right direction, or maybe you know of someone who can help.

Compassion is something you learn from your own suffering. Can you think of a time when someone showed you compassion? How did it make you feel? Ask God to help you use your own troubles to be helpful and caring toward others.

Lord God, no one likes to suffer. But it's good to know I can use my own troubles to be compassionate, sympathetic, and loving. Amen.

JUDGE FAIRLY

"Be fair in how you judge. Do not show favor to the poor or to the great. Be fair in how you judge your neighbor."
LEVITICUS 19:15

Jesus warns us to be careful when judging others. He says, "Do not say what is wrong in other people's lives. Then other people will not say what is wrong in your life" (Matthew 7:1). "Do not say a person is guilty by what you see. Be sure you know when you say what is right or wrong" (John 7:24). Jesus reminds us to be fair when judging others.

Everyone messes up. We all behave badly. It's easy to notice what others do wrong, but we need to remember we aren't perfect either. God doesn't judge people by what they look like, where they live, or how popular they are. He judges by what's inside their hearts, their actions, and whether or not they choose to follow Him.

God's judgments are always right and fair. God made you in His image, so He expects your judgments to be right and fair too.

Dear God, lead me to seeing the good in others. Help me to judge them fairly. Amen.

HAVE MERCY

*"Those who show loving-kindness are happy,
because they will have loving-kindness shown to them."*
MATTHEW 5:7

Can you think of a time you messed up and your parents could have punished you, but instead they showed you mercy? *Mercy* means loving-kindness. Your parents had the authority to punish you, but because you were sorry, they were merciful.

God is merciful too. He has power to punish us when we mess up and displease Him, but instead, when we are sorry, He is kind and forgiving. God always wants you to show mercy toward those who mess up and seek forgiveness.

If a friend said something unkind to you and then she apologized, how could you show her some mercy? Jesus says, "Those who show loving-kindness are happy, because they will have loving-kindness shown to them." Mercy is important because it reminds us we mess up just like everyone else. Mercy reminds us to judge others fairly.

Father God, You have been merciful and shown me loving-kindness again and again. Help me to be merciful to others the way You are merciful to me. Amen.

ADVENTUROUS

You will show me the way of life. Being with You is to be full of joy. In Your right hand there is happiness forever.
PSALM 16:11

Are you a girl who loves adventures? God wants you to seek out and experience His world. He put many wonderful things there for you to explore, things that will bring you joy. Where would you like to go? What would you like to do? Have you set your sights on climbing a mountain? Traveling in space? Exploring Antarctica or the Amazon rain forest?

Big adventures start with little adventures. Each adventure leads to learning new skills, practicing what you learn, using good sense, and staying safe. Let God be your guide. Be watchful for ideas He puts in your head for new things you might try. Ask Him to lead where He wants you to go; ask what He wants you to see. With each new adventure, you will learn more about Him—and yourself.

God, let's travel through life together. Where do You want me to go? What do You want me to learn and see? Be my guide, Lord. Let's go! Amen.

BRAVE

He gives strength to the weak. And He gives power to him who has little strength.
ISAIAH 40:29

Have you ever felt small in a big world? God can give you courage! He knew that from your little years on, you would need to be brave.

First times often require bravery. Maybe when you were very little you went to day care. Can you remember being brave the first time Mom or Dad left you there? The bravery you learned from that experience helped you to be brave on your first day of school. As you lean on God's strength, you will learn you can trust Him. With each new experience, God will increase your bravery. He will use His own power working through you to make you strong.

Name a situation when you felt afraid but you bravely faced your fear and it turned out okay. God was with you, helping you. He was with you then, and you can count on Him helping you to be brave throughout your entire life.

Dear God, I am able to be brave because I have your power working through me. When I am weak, you make me strong. Amen.

THE GREAT CREATOR

*In the beginning God made from nothing
the heavens and the earth.*

GENESIS 1:1

Imagine making something from nothing. That would be impossible, wouldn't it? But that's exactly what God did. Amazingly, He made His ideas become real by speaking things into being!

God created the heavens, what we can see and everything beyond, and a universe we can only imagine. He created the earth, water, plants, animals, people—and YOU. When God created us, He gave us many of the same qualities He has, things like patience, kindness, and the ability to love and forgive. God also gave us some of His creative skills, the ability to think, reason, work, and make things.

Wherever you are right now, look around you. Someone created everything you see. Those creations began with an idea. Often other people stepped in to help make that idea happen. They designed and built those things you see, and they did it using the skills God gave them.

Dear God. You are the Great Creator. You've given me some of your creative skills. so please Bless me with good ideas so I can create things too. Amen.

CREATIVE FLAIR

Whatever work you do, do it with all your heart. Do it for the Lord and not for men.
COLOSSIANS 3:23

Your creativity pleases God—it can come in many different forms: art and crafts, building and fixing things, writing, inventing things, making music, dancing, acting, cooking, baking, sewing, photography, gardening. . .

God made each of us to be different, so we create in different ways. At an art show, you won't see any two pieces of art that are alike. That's an example of how creativity works. It begins with a thought in someone's head, then the person takes that thought and makes it into something people can experience or see.

God made us to be creative so we can add good things to His world. When using our creativity, we should be careful to honor God with everything we create. Think about this: Does a song filled with swear words honor God? How about a poem that makes fun of someone?

Lord, You made me to be creative. Guide me to use my creativity in ways that please and honor You. Amen.

HAVE A LITTLE FUN!

Let them praise His name with dancing. Let them sing praises to Him with timbrels and a harp.

PSALM 149:3

Take a break today and do something creative and fun. Write a poem. Make up a song. Create a new game to play. Draw or paint a picture. Bake a cake. Play dress-up with your baby sister. Build something with your little brother. Make a video with your friends.

God wants you to love Him, obey Him, and please Him with everything you do, but He also wants you to have fun. What is your favorite way of having fun? Maybe it's a family game night, playing a sport, going to a park, swimming at the local pool, teaching your dog new tricks, or just hanging out with your friends. The Bible says Jesus came to give us a great, full life (John 10:10). Fun is part of life. Fun is good as long as it's God-pleasing fun.

- -

Dear God, I'm grateful you have put so many ways to have fun in your world. Guide me. What should I make or do today? Amen.

RESOURCEFUL

*She looks for wool and flax, and works with
willing hands. She is like ships that trade.
She brings her food from far away.*
PROVERBS 31:13–14

Resourcefulness is using your skills, imagination, and creativity to solve problems. Proverbs 31:13–14 is an example of what it means to be resourceful.

If someone needed a coat, hat, gloves, blanket, or anything else made of cloth, and she had none, she could look for wool or other material to make something. Or if there was no food nearby, she could think of ways to get some. God wants you to be resourceful. He put all kinds of things in the world you can use to make other things. (How many things could you do with an empty milk jug?) God put people and tools in the world to help with your resourcefulness.

If you don't know how to fix something, where can you go to find out? If you need to call your mom and the phone's battery is dead, what could you do? Practice being resourceful today.

Dear God, teach me to Be resourceful
By using my imagination,
creativity, and skills. Amen.

BENDING BETTER

Be gentle and kind. Do not be hard on others.
Let love keep you from doing that.
EPHESIANS 4:2

How flexible are you? Maybe dancing is the first thing that comes to mind, the ability to easily bend your arms and legs. That's one definition of flexible. But there's another. *Flexible* also means the willingness to change or compromise. God can help you learn to adjust your behavior to fit the circumstances. It's movie night at your house. You and your sister want different films. You could argue about it or compromise.

Compromise means choosing a movie you both like, or you could decide one of you gets to choose tonight and the other next time. Being flexible also means creating new ideas when you can't have what you want. Your family planned a picnic, but it rained. You could stay home feeling sad or—what else? Compromise and flexibility take practice. It helps to be gentle and kind toward others and do what pleases God.

Father, when I can't have what I want, help me to be willing to compromise or change. Amen.

OVERCOMER

*Every child of God has power over the sins
of the world. The way we have power over
the sins of the world is by our faith.*

1 JOHN 5:4

When you are a child of God, you have His power working through you to *overcome*—to take control of—any trouble that gets in your way. God gave you a powerful tool to use against trouble: faith. When you trust that God controls the world, you know He has power over every kind of difficulty. With God's power working through you, you can take control of your problems. Ask God to grow your courage. Whether you're fighting a battle with your health, or trouble with kids at school, struggling with a subject in class, or trying to reach a goal, remember you aren't fighting the battle alone. God is with you. He is always working for your good. Choose your attitude. Choose to be obedient, courageous, and strong. Have faith that God will help with whatever trouble gets in your way.

Dear God, together we can overcome my troubles.
Help me to trust You with all my heart. Amen.

EVERYONE WELCOME

*"When you have a supper, ask poor people.
Ask those who cannot walk and those who are blind."*
LUKE 14:13

Everyone on earth has something in common: God made us all. He loves each and every one of us enough to send Jesus to die for our sins.

God made us to love each other too. He doesn't want anyone left out because they are poor, have a disability, or struggle with certain skills. He doesn't want anyone left out because of how they look. Maybe you know someone who is often excluded. Jesus reminds us to include those people in our plans. The Bible says Jesus noticed those who were left out, and He welcomed them.

Friendship is important to everybody, and God made you to be a good friend. What are some activities you could plan with a friend who can't walk? How about a friend who can't see? A friend whose family is new to your country? Everyone is welcome in God's family. What are some ways your family could welcome someone who is left out?

Dear God, guide me to notice those who are left out. I will invite them to Be my friends. Amen.

I AM GOD'S MASTERPIECE

But now, O Lord, You are our Father.
We are the clay, and You are our pot maker.
All of us are the work of Your hand.

ISAIAH 64:8

At an art show you can buy all kinds of art, each piece priced at what the artist decides it is worth. But the art in the world's greatest museums isn't for sale. It is art created by the world's best artists, *masterpieces*—representing the artists' best work—one-of-a-kind art pieces that cannot be replaced. Masterpieces are priceless, worth more than money can buy.

Do you know you are God's masterpiece? God made you, and He is the greatest artist of all. His work is perfect. God made you a one-of-a-kind piece of art. You (and all of His children) are His best work. You are priceless and irreplaceable.

There is, and always ever will be, one and only YOU. God wants you to handle yourself as His masterpiece, and that means liking who you are and taking good care of yourself.

Dear heavenly Father, I am the work of Your hands, Your best work, and I will take good care of ME. Amen.

JUST LIKE JESUS

*Do as God would do. Much-loved children
want to do as their fathers do.*

EPHESIANS 5:1

Everyone wants to be well liked. But some girls want to be popular. They want others to notice how pretty they are, or how smart, or talented, or how important. They want to be the leader and have other girls follow them. That's not how God wants you to treat others.

He wants you to be kind, caring, compassionate, helpful, honest, trustworthy, and faithful—like Jesus. He didn't make you to be popular. He made you to be likeable by doing what He would do and behaving in ways that please Him. It isn't important to God how many friends you have or how popular you are. Instead He wants you to be a friend and have friends for the right reasons.

You don't need to impress people, just treat them as Jesus would. You are the one-of-a kind masterpiece God created. When choosing your friends, choose those who like you just because you are YOU—a beautiful child of God.

Dear God, if I think I'd like to be more popular,
like some of the other girls, remind me
it's more important that I'm likeable—
and for all the right reasons. Amen.

UNIQUE GIFTS

God has given each of you a gift. Use it to help each other. This will show God's loving-favor.
1 PETER 4:10

Your skills and talents. . .the experiences you've had. . .the places you've been. . .what you've heard and seen. . .your culture and heritage. . .the history of your ancestors. . .all of these things are God's gifts to you. They make you unique.

They make you interesting too. Your life story is different from everyone else's. How you view and interact with the world is different from other people. When you share your stories, ideas, thoughts, and experiences with others, you can help them see the world through your eyes. What you share might lead them to explore their own God-given gifts.

How can you do that? By telling your friends what you know about who God is and why He loves us. They might find that interesting too!

Dear God, the gifts You've given me—my experiences in life and my talents and skills—make me interesting and unique. Lead me to use my gifts to help others. Amen.

SO MANY SMARTS

An understanding mind gets much learning,
and the ear of the wise listens for much learning.
PROVERBS 18:15

What does it mean to be smart? For some girls it means being super-good in all their subjects at school and getting excellent grades. But people are smart in different ways. It's another of those things that make them unique.

It's smart to work hard at being the best you can be with the gifts God gave you. It's smart to be willing to learn and to ask for help when you don't understand. Smart is keeping at it when something is hard.

It's not good to measure how smart you are against your classmates. God gave you things you are good at. He also gave you the ability to learn. Focus on learning. Work at becoming better as you learn. And if ever you feel you don't measure up, talk with God about it. He used people who didn't think they were smart to do some pretty amazing things.

Father God, help me never to think I'm not smart enough. It's enough that I work hard, do my best, and am willing to learn. Amen.

BUT, LORD, I AM NOT...

Moses said to the Lord, "Lord, I am not a man of words. I have never been. . . . For I am slow in talking and it is difficult for me to speak."
EXODUS 4:10

God's people, the Israelites, were slaves in Egypt. God chose a man named Moses to talk with Egypt's leader, Pharaoh, and demand he let God's people go. Moses didn't think he was good enough. "Lord," he said, "I am not a man of words. . . . It is difficult for me to speak." But God had already chosen Moses as the one. God knew He could work through Moses. Moses obeyed God. He told Pharaoh, "Let God's people go!" Then Moses led the people out of Egypt to a land God promised them. God made Moses a great leader.

If ever you think you are not smart enough, strong enough, or able to be used by God, He says, "Yes, you are!" He can take everything you think you are not and turn it around. He can even lead you to do great things.

Lord, when I think of what I am not, remind me of who You are. Amen.

ALWAYS JOYFUL

*A glad heart makes a happy face, but when
the heart is sad, the spirit is broken.*
PROVERBS 15:13

God wants you to have a glad heart, an inner joy, that you can share with others. When you spread your joy around, it makes people smile.

What makes you fun to be with? Are you the first to suggest something fun for you and your friends to enjoy? Do you have a good sense of humor? Do you love entertaining others by singing, dancing, acting, or using other talents? You can probably think of many other reasons you are fun to be around.

Part of being a joyful person is having a positive attitude toward life that comes from knowing God—like the ability to laugh at yourself if something silly or unexpected happens to you. Are you able to do that? When you see humor in your own circumstances, it shows others you are a good sport. If you make it your goal to make others happy, it will make you a happier person too.

Dear God, thank you for filling my heart with gladness. Wherever I go, help me to use it and share it. Amen.

A GOOD SPORT

I have fought a good fight. I have finished the
work I was to do. I have kept the faith.
2 TIMOTHY 4:7

A good sport is humble. She doesn't think she is more important than her opponent. When she wins a game, she congratulates the other player for playing well. Can you think of a few things you could say to your opponent if you won the game?

Everyone wants to win when they play, but winning doesn't always happen. A good sport is respectful when she loses. She is courteous, kind, and pleasant. She congratulates her opponent for the win. Competing isn't all about winning. It's about finishing the game knowing you have done your best and you've honored God by the way you played.

God wants you to be a good sport. Whether or not you have a strong body and a sharp mind, or are running a race or playing chess, you honor Him by being a good sport whether you win or lose the game.

Dear God, I play to win. But whether I win or lose, I will do my best to be a good sport. Amen.

CHALLENGE YOURSELF

I am sure that God Who began the good work in you will keep on working in you until the day Jesus Christ comes again.
PHILIPPIANS 1:6

I challenge you to a game of checkers! I challenge you to a race!

Whatever the game, a challenge can be fun. There's another kind of challenge though—challenging yourself to become an even better version of YOU. It requires willingness to change things about yourself.

Change can be hard. It takes work. Maybe you want to become more comfortable speaking or performing for an audience. Your challenge could be finding ways to build your confidence. You might practice first in front of your family, then for a small group of friends, then finally work your way toward performing on stage and loving it!

God has put many challenges in His life plan for you. With each new challenge, you will learn to overcome obstacles that get in your way. For every challenge you conquer, you will learn and grow. What is the biggest challenge you face right now?

Heavenly Father, whatever the challenge, I trust You to help me through it. Amen.

TAKE CARE

*Do you not know that your body is a house
of God where the Holy Spirit lives?
God gave you His Holy Spirit. Now you belong
to God. You do not belong to yourselves.*
1 CORINTHIANS 6:19

God made your body, but it's up to you to take care of it. You've learned that God is with you all the time. His Spirit lives inside you in that hidden part of your heart, the part that guides you and tells you right from wrong. When you care for your body, you are also caring for the place where God lives.

Caring for your body means making healthy choices. Your body is the only one you have here on earth, and to be healthy, it needs exercise, rest, water, and the right kinds of food. You should also treat your body with respect. When you respect your body, you are showing respect for the one who created it—God. Your body is important to Him. Everything you do to your body and with it should honor Him.

Dear God, I will honor You By caring for my Body and treating it with respect. Amen.

KEEP IT NEAT!

*All things should be done in the right
way, one after the other.*
1 CORINTHIANS 14:40

Your mom says, "Did you clean your room? Did you put things back where they belong?" Did you, or are you putting off that task as long as you can?

Keeping things neat and organized might not seem important, but 1 Corinthians 14:40 in the Bible reminds us that all things should be done in the right way, one after the other. Remember, God made us in His image. When He created everything, He did it in an orderly way. After God finished creating earth, He made a man, Adam, and God gave Adam the job of caring for what He had made. (Read about it in Genesis 1:1–2:15.)

You have the same job God assigned to Adam. God expects you to care for everything He's given you. You show respect for God and honor Him by keeping your room and your things organized, neat, and clean.

Father, I didn't know keeping my stuff neat and organized honors you. Thank you for all you've given me. I will try harder to keep it neat and clean. Amen.

GOD'S WORLD, MY WORLD

The earth is the Lord's, and all that is in it, the world, and all who live in it.

PSALM 24:1

Long before He made you, God created everything on earth. Just as you are a masterpiece created by God, so is the earth. It's an amazing creation, a true, priceless work of art.

Now imagine this: What if you created a beautiful painting or other work of art, put it on display, and then a bunch of people came along and messed up what you'd created? They threw junk on it and covered it up with all kinds of ugliness. How would that make you feel?

When people don't care about the earth, it's like they're messing up God's masterpiece. If you're a girl who loves God and cares about His things, it will be important to you to care for His earth. Can you think of several ways you and your friends can help keep the earth neat and clean? Put those ideas into action.

Dear God, You made Earth my home. You made it a Beautiful place to live, and I will do my part to help keep it clean. Amen.

WHAT I WEAR

*I also want the women to dress modestly,
with decency and propriety, adorning themselves,
not with elaborate hairstyles or gold or pearls or
expensive clothes, but with good deeds, appropriate
for women who profess to worship God.*
1 TIMOTHY 2:9–10 NIV

Styles change. How we dress today is very different from when Jesus' follower, Paul, wrote about fashion in 1 Timothy 2:9–10. God wants you, and all of us, to dress in ways that honor Him. That means different things to different people.

We all have our own styles and ideas about what is okay. But it's important to decide if what we wear is pleasing to God. Would it honor Him to wear T-shirts with slogans that use bad language or make fun of people? Would it honor Him to wear a devil costume to a dress-up party? Maybe you are a fashionista, a girl with her own, unique style. That's great! Just keep in mind that God sees what you wear, and you should always dress to honor Him.

Dear God, when I create my own style, I will think about what I wear and dress to please You. Amen.

SLEEP WELL

I will lie down and sleep in peace.
O Lord, You alone keep me safe.
PSALM 4:8

Part of taking good care of your mind and body is getting enough sleep. Sleep recharges your body and brain so you will be rested when you begin the next day. Most scientists recommend kids your age get nine to twelve hours of sleep every day.

That seems like a lot, doesn't it? But recharging your mind and body takes time. People, and animals too, need sleep to survive. Without a good night's sleep, you become tired and grumpy. Go a long time without sleep, and your brain doesn't think well. A poor night's sleep can affect how well you do in school. Sleep is important.

Maybe sometimes you don't fall asleep quickly because your thoughts and worries keep you awake. When God saved you, He promised to be with you always. God never sleeps. He is up all night, and He is everywhere. Give your thoughts and worries to Him. When you end your prayers tonight, use the words of Psalm 4:8. . .

Dear Lord, I will lie down and sleep in peace because I know You keep me safe. Amen.

MY SUPERPOWER

We do not use those things to fight with that the world uses. We use the things God gives to fight with and they have power. Those things God gives to fight with destroy the strong-places of the devil.

2 CORINTHIANS 10:4

You've been thinking about everything that makes you YOU. God made you unique, special, and one of a kind. But He also gave you something you share with all who believe in and trust Him. God gave you some of His power.

Whenever you need strength to reach a goal, solve a problem, or stand up to anything evil that gets in your way, you have God's power working within you. You can tap into that power by asking God for help and by trusting Him to make you strong and brave. God's power is your superpower!

No, you won't be able to fly, or have X-ray vision, or become invisible like those fake superheroes in the movies. But you will have the amazing powers of wisdom, strength, patience, and perseverance that only come from God.

Father God, thank You for giving me some of Your power. Teach me to use it well. Amen.

MY WEAKNESSES

He answered me, "I am all you need. I give you My
loving-favor. My power works best in weak people."
2 CORINTHIANS 12:9

As you've thought about everything that makes you unique, special, and one of a kind, you might have noticed a few things you'd like to improve. Everyone has weaknesses. Maybe you've caught yourself being a little gossipy, jealous, lazy, or thinking you are better than someone else. Maybe you space out sometimes and daydream when you should be concentrating on learning at school, or you are stubborn, impatient, or a tiny bit bossy. Maybe you don't always obey your parents.

The Bible says God's power works best in weak people. That means if you decide to change something about yourself, God will give you power to do it. Identifying your weaknesses is a good thing. As you work on them, you will become a stronger and even better version of you. What are your weaknesses? What about yourself would you like to change? Ask God to help you.

Dear God, help me identify those things about myself You want me to improve. Then give me power to do it. Amen.

WHEN I AM WEAK I'M STRONG

I receive joy when I am weak. I receive joy when people talk against me and make it hard for me and try to hurt me and make trouble for me. I receive joy when all these things come to me because of Christ. For when I am weak, then I am strong.

2 CORINTHIANS 12:10

Are you joyful when people say bad things about you, make it hard for you, hurt you, or make trouble for you? Jesus' follower, Paul, said he felt joyful in those circumstances because it brought him nearer to Jesus.

For Paul, joy was the inner peace he felt when trouble knocked him down. If he didn't feel strong enough to overcome his troubles, Paul was certain he could tap into Jesus' power for strength. He knew Jesus would help him and make him strong enough to stand up to whatever trouble came his way.

Jesus will do the same for you. Whenever you feel weak, you are strong because Jesus is your strength.

. . . .

Dear Jesus, when I feel too weak to stand up to my troubles, I will rely on Your power to make me strong. Amen.

GOOD THOUGHTS AND LIES

Hear me and answer me. My thoughts trouble me and I have no peace.
PSALM 55:2

God wants you to think good thoughts and to have hope. He doesn't want you to worry but to have peace.

Like most people, you'll sometimes be troubled by your thoughts. The devil likes to create a war of thoughts inside us. He wants the thoughts he puts in our heads to keep us from the kind of thinking God wants us to have. Thoughts that come from the devil are lies. They take away the confidence we have in ourselves because we know God. They make us feel worried, anxious, and afraid.

When thoughts like that enter your mind, tell them, "Stop!" You are not your thoughts. You are who God says you are. God will never say you are not pretty enough, smart enough, or good enough. He will tell you He loves you. God says He will guide you and help you.

Think about your thoughts today. Where do they come from?

Lord God, help me to recognize thoughts that are lies. Replace them with thoughts you want me to have— thoughts of hope and peace. Amen.

BE HOPEFUL

Be happy in your hope. Do not give up when trouble comes. Do not let anything stop you from praying.
ROMANS 12:12

Hope is expecting something good in the future. When you say, "I hope we have tacos for lunch," it's like saying, "I wish we'd have tacos." But we don't always get what we wish for.

A different kind of hope exists, a hope you can always trust in, a hope that God put inside your heart. Hope in Him means trusting that God will do exactly what He has promised. You can always expect something good from God, but it might not come exactly as you want it.

You can trust in your hope that God loves you. You can trust in your hope that God is working out your problems and that He is with you in trouble. You can trust in your hope that God listens and hears your prayers. Hoping in God makes you happy because you know He will never let you down.

Dear God, my hope is in You. I trust in all Your promises and in Your goodness and love. Amen.

HOW MUCH AM I WORTH?

"Are not five small birds sold for two small pieces of money? God does not forget even one of the birds. . . . You are worth more than many small birds."
LUKE 12:6–7

God made you to be His. He didn't make you to be bought or sold. He would never put a price tag on you. You are His unique creation, His special girl. You are worth more to God than all the money in the world, all the gold, all the precious gems.

You are His. He created you to be part of His family, and He also gave you a family here on earth to love you and help you grow. Do you see yourself the way God does? You should never measure your worth against how much you think you need to improve, or your age, or how you look. You shouldn't measure your worth against what others think of you either. Only measure your worth against what God thinks of you. To Him, you are priceless. You are His, now and forever.

Heavenly Father, thank You for making me special, important, and priceless. Amen.

GOD GIVES ME GRACE

But by the grace of God I am what I am.
1 CORINTHIANS 15:10 NIV

Maybe you have heard your pastor or Sunday school teacher speak about God's grace. *Grace* means receiving God's blessings even when we don't deserve them. Grace is a part of God's character.

We all mess up and displease God, but if we are sorry He forgives us. God doesn't keep score of how often we mess up. He doesn't withhold His blessings from us because we have sinned. God gives us grace because we are precious to Him.

Remember all the good things God does for you. Think of the wonderful ways He makes you YOU. God blessed you with His goodness on the day He created you, and He will continue blessing you all the days of your life. At night before you go to sleep, think about your blessings. When you say your bedtime prayers, thank God for His grace. Thank Him for blessing you.

Dear God, I am not worthy of Your grace and Your Blessings. But You give them to me anyway. Thank You for Being so good to me. Amen.

GOD SAYS, "COME BACK!"

Return to the Lord your God, for He is full of loving-kindness and loving-pity. He is slow to anger, full of love, and ready to keep His punishment from you.

JOEL 2:13

Sometimes we go our own way and forget about God. We mess up and are sorry.

Jesus told about a boy whose dad gave him some money. The boy left home and spent it all foolishly. Soon he was broke, hungry, tired, and he wanted to go home. He was sorry for what he had done. The boy wanted to apologize to his dad, but he worried about how his dad would react. When he got home, his dad was so happy to see him that he threw his son a homecoming party.

Jesus told this story (found in Luke 15:11–32) to remind us that if we turn away from God, He wants us to come back. He will welcome us back! So if you've put a little space between you and God, go back to Him. He misses you, and He forgives you.

Dear God. I'm sorry I've drifted away. I want to come back. I know you will welcome me and forgive me. Amen.

GROWING AND CHANGING

You have now become a new person and are always learning more about Christ. You are being made more like Christ. He is the One Who made you.
COLOSSIANS 3:10

As you've thought about how God created you and how He is working in your life, have you noticed you are growing and changing? When you put your faith and trust in God, He helps you to become more like Him. God has provided Jesus as your teacher and the Bible as your guide.

It's time for another checkup. How has your behavior changed for the better? Maybe you are more patient, kind, forgiving. . .

- Name something you are able to do now you couldn't do a year ago.
- Name something new you have learned about yourself.
- Name something you have done that made you feel more confident and brave.

How has your relationship with God changed in the past year? Do you feel closer to Him? Each day, with God's help, you are growing, changing, and becoming a new person.

Thank You, Lord, for guiding me
as I grow and change. Amen.

BETTER AND BETTER

*I can do all things because Christ
gives me the strength.*
PHILIPPIANS 4:13

Girl, look at how much you have grown and changed! It's not just your body that is growing and changing. More importantly, it's the part that makes you YOU.

God, your Creator and heavenly Father, is helping you to grow in confidence—confidence in Him and in yourself. Your faith in Him is growing. You are growing to become more compassionate and merciful. You judge more fairly now and are better at welcoming new kids into your circle of friends. You are learning to challenge yourself and overcome obstacles. You are braver and more willing to try new things. You are more organized and more aware of keeping God's world neat and clean. You are taking better care of your body.

The Bible says, "I can do all things because Christ gives me the strength." Each day, with His help, you are getting better and better at becoming the girl God wants you to be.

Dear God, inside my heart I can feel myself
growing and changing. I'm discovering
more about who I am and who
You want me to be. Amen.

BUT I'M NOT PERFECT!

"You must be perfect as your Father
in heaven is perfect."
MATTHEW 5:48

Jesus was speaking to a huge crowd, teaching them about how God wanted them to behave. (It's called the Sermon on the Mount, and you can read more about it in Matthew 5–7.) He taught about anger and forgiveness, helping and loving each other, how to pray, having faith in God, and many other things. Jesus said, "You must be perfect as your Father in heaven is perfect."

You might think, *But I'm not perfect. I can't be perfect!* And you're right. No one is perfect, and no one will ever be as perfect as God. What Jesus meant is we should try. We should do our best to behave the way God wants us to. Each day we should work toward the goal of becoming more like Him.

No, you're not perfect. But God loves you anyway. He loves you just as you are today. God knows you are trying, in His strength, and that is enough for Him.

. . . .

Dear God. when You made me, You knew I would never Be perfect. But You promised to love me anyway. I love You too. Amen.

GOD THINKS ABOUT ME

*Your thoughts are of great worth to me,
O God. How many there are!*
PSALM 139:17

Do you know God thinks about you? He thought about you even before He created you and before you were born. God is thinking about you right now.

Not a minute goes by that He doesn't have you in His thoughts. God knows better than anyone else who you are right now and who you will become as you grow older. He is always thinking of the best ways to guide and help you. He is thinking about the situations you face with strength and those where you need to be stronger. He is thinking about the people in your life who can help you, those who are with you today and those you will meet in the future. God is thinking about your prayers, what you've asked Him for, and what you need. God is always thinking about how much He loves you.

He knows the plans He has for you; He knows you are able, and He believes in you.

Father God, knowing that you always think of me makes me feel safe and loved. Amen.

"LORD, I HAVE FAITH!"

"Lord, I have faith. Help my weak faith to be stronger!"
MARK 9:24

Do you have faith that, with God's help, you can do great things? God created you to have faith in Him and faith in the ability He's given you. You've discovered that with His strength working through you, God enables you to accomplish more than you ever thought you could.

Faith isn't a feeling. It's an attitude of trusting that God is thinking of you, guiding you, loving you, and helping you with all your challenges and problems—even when you don't feel it. Faith is also trusting in your abilities beyond your expectations, believing that God can work through you to accomplish His plans.

Everyone's faith is sometimes weak. When we don't see God working things out for us we wonder where He is. When we work toward a goal, we might doubt we have enough faith in ourselves to reach it. When that happens we should say to God, "Lord, help my weak faith to be stronger!"

Lord God, thank you for reminding me faith is an attitude. Strengthen my faith in you and also in my ability. Amen.

THE POPULAR GIRL

*We do not compare ourselves with those who
think they are good. They compare themselves
with themselves. They decide what they think
is good or bad and compare themselves
with those ideas. They are foolish.*
2 CORINTHIANS 10:12

Maybe you know a girl who is super popular. Other girls try to dress and talk like her. They compare themselves to her and want to be just like her. Sometimes you might wish you were just like her too.

But winning popularity contests, being the one everyone wants to dress and talk like, isn't so important to God. Instead He wants you to be liked for your good behavior. God made you to be an example of what it's like to follow Him. He wants the ways you are kind, unselfish, caring, and helpful to lead others to follow Him too.

When you catch yourself wishing you were that popular girl, stop and remember God didn't make you to be like her. God made you to be like YOU.

Dear God, remind me not to compare myself
to those who are super popular.
I'm fine just as I am. Amen.

WHAT OTHERS THINK OF ME

It is dangerous to be concerned with what others think of you, but if you trust the LORD, you are safe.
PROVERBS 29:25 GNT

Maybe you have a friend who is always telling you what you shouldn't do. "You shouldn't wear that color. You shouldn't wear that hairstyle. You shouldn't be friends with those kids," or even "You shouldn't talk so much about God and Jesus."

What others say can build you up or cut you down. It can be dangerous to change yourself to fit in with what someone says you should do. Instead of being concerned about what your friends say, it is more important to remember who God says you are and to think of all the good ways He made you YOU.

Kind and caring friends might sometimes offer wise advice about something you could improve. Ask God to help you know the difference between good and bad advice. Never think less of yourself because of what someone says to you.

Dear God, instead of Believing what others say aBout me, help me to think of myself as You think of me. Amen.

I WANT TO BELONG

We are His work. He has made us to belong
to Christ Jesus so we can work for Him.
He planned that we should do this.
EPHESIANS 2:10

Everyone wants to feel like they belong. When meeting a new group of people, we look for those in the group who will welcome and include us. Belonging makes us feel safe and secure. It assures us we are with people who will guide and help us.

Do you know where you belong most? You belong with Jesus. God made you to belong to Jesus and to know Him as your helper and friend. When you belong to Jesus, you don't have to feel alone in a group because Jesus is always with you. You can ask Him to guide you to those who are most likely to welcome you.

Maybe you've just become part of a new group, but you don't feel comfortable and welcome yet. When you say your prayers today, ask Jesus to help you.

Dear Jesus, When I'm with a new group of people, I don't always feel like I Belong. Please guide me to those who will welcome and include me. Amen.

WHERE DO I FIT IN?

Do not be joined together with those who do not belong to Christ. How can that which is good get along with that which is bad? How can light be in the same place with darkness?

2 CORINTHIANS 6:14

When working a jigsaw puzzle, sometimes there's a piece that looks like it should fit, but it doesn't. If that sounds like you, you could be trying to fit in with the wrong crowd.

Have you discovered you don't have much in common with the girls you hang out with? It could be their ideas about what's right and wrong seem different from yours and they don't know Christ—Jesus—like you do.

God made you to fit in with those who know and love Him. The Bible warns about getting too close with those who don't know Jesus or disrespect Him. The danger is you could mess up and become more like them. When making new friends, look for those who know and love Him. Usually you can tell who they are by the way they behave.

Dear Jesus, lead me to the friends you want me to have, friends who will draw me nearer to you. Amen.

I WANT TO BE ACCEPTED

Accept one another, then, just as Christ accepted you, in order to bring praise to God.
ROMANS 15:7 NIV

Every child is precious to God. He made you, and all His children, to be loved and accepted—to be welcomed just as they are. Do you know that Jesus invited all the children to come to Him? He told His disciples, "Let the little children come to Me. Do not try to stop them. The holy nation of God is made up of ones like these" (Luke 18:16). Jesus accepted all the children. None were turned away.

Do you know kids who are often excluded? It could be because they are new at school, because of how they look, where they come from, where they live, or for other reasons. What could you do to include them? Everyone deserves to be accepted just as they are. If you ever feel left out, ask Jesus to lead you to good, caring friends who will welcome you.

Dear Jesus, You want every child to feel included. You've always accepted me. I will do my best to be like You and welcome those whom others leave out. Amen.

I WANT GOOD FRIENDS

A friend loves at all times.
PROVERBS 17:17

When God created you, He planned for Jesus to be your friend. God knew if you accepted Jesus' friendship, you would have the best friend ever, a perfect forever friend, one you could always count on.

God planned for you to have other friends too, good friends who would accept you just as you are, help you when you need it, and forgive you when you mess up. Here are several things to think about when choosing your friends:

- Do they leave others out?
- Do they provide help and comfort when times are hard?
- Are they encouragers, or do they judge others and cut them down?
- Would God approve of their behavior?
- Do they know and love Jesus?

Good friends are a blessing, a gift from God!

Dear God, throughout my life, I will make new friends. Guide me to those who will encourage me and stay with me in good times and in bad. Amen.

I WANT TO BE RESPECTED

Let no one show little respect for you because you are young. Show other Christians how to live by your life. They should be able to follow you in the way you talk and in what you do. Show them how to live in faith and in love and in holy living.

1 TIMOTHY 4:12

Imagine this: You try to set a good example. You try to do what's right. You behave and talk in ways that please God, and you aren't shy about sharing your faith and telling others about Jesus. But some of the girls make fun of and disrespect you for living as God says you should. What would you do? Would you continue behaving to please God, or would you choose to be more like those other girls?

You deserve respect. When friends disrespect you for doing what's right, it's best to walk away and leave them alone. If they disrespect you for being YOU, they aren't good friends. Pray for them. Ask God to guide them closer to Him.

Dear Lord, I deserve respect for following You. Please help those who hurt me. Lead them to know You. Amen.

I WANT TO FEEL LOVED

*We have come to know and believe the
love God has for us. God is love.*
1 JOHN 4:16

The Bible tells us that God is love. When He created you, God made you with love. He won't ever stop loving you when you mess up and need forgiveness. He won't ever leave you. God wants us to love each other with His kind of love, a love that is true, caring, and forgiving. Everyone wants to feel loved.

We can have days, though, when we feel lonely and wonder if anyone loves us. It is important not to hold on to those feelings. To chase them away, we can remember God loves us with His perfect love all the time. We can remember Jesus loves us so much He gave His life so we could live forever in heaven. We can also think of family members, friends, teachers, and others who have treated us in kind and loving ways. Love is all around us if only we look for it.

Dear God, you love me. you made me to
be loved. Please open my eyes to all the
love you've put around me. Amen.

141

I WANT TO FEEL SAFE

As for me, I will call on God and the Lord will save me. I will cry out and complain in the evening and morning and noon, and He will hear my voice.

PSALM 55:16–17

The Bible says David was afraid while running away from King Saul who wanted to hurt him. He told God he wished he were a bird so he could fly to a safe place far away from his enemies.

But then David remembered God was his safe place. He trusted God to bring him through his trouble. David knew he could pray all night and all day, and God would hear and help him. Trusting God made David feel safe even when trouble was all around him.

God wants you to feel safe too by trusting in Him as your safe place. Whatever trouble you face, you can trust that God is with you, and He will lead you through it.

Father, you will bring me through any trouble that comes my way. I know I am safe because you are with me. Amen.

I WANT TO FEEL CALM

*May the Lord of peace give you His peace
at all times. The Lord be with you all.*
2 THESSALONIANS 3:16

God wants you to have a sense of peace—the ability to know everything will be okay because He is in control and He is with you. But sometimes it's hard to find that peace inside our hearts. We're unsure of many things, and not knowing what will happen makes us feel anxious. You might not always know why you feel anxious, nervous, and even a little afraid, but you want those feelings to go away. You want to feel calm. Don't worry. You haven't lost the peace God put inside your heart. It's still there waiting for you to take hold of it. Pray about it. When you feel anxious, talk about it with a grownup. And remember, most of the time what you worry about won't happen, and if it does, God will bring you through it.

Dear God. I don't like this anxious feeling. Help me find the peace you put inside my heart. Remind me that everything will be okay because I'm with you. Amen.

TRUTH OR LIES?

"The devil has nothing to do with the truth. There is no truth in him. It is expected of the devil to lie, for he is a liar and the father of lies."

JOHN 8:44

The devil loves to confuse people by telling them lies. That's why God gave us the Bible. It's filled with God's truth. If we know what's in there, we can recognize the devil's lies.

Do you know the devil can make your feelings lie to you by putting false ideas inside your head? He says things like "You're not good enough or smart enough or strong enough." The more you think about his lies, the worse you'll feel about yourself and your abilities.

God wants you to know the truth. Every word in the Bible is true, and you can trust everything it says about God, about you, and how He wants you to live. If your thoughts lead you not to feel good about yourself, think about your feelings and compare them to the Bible's truth.

Father, help me to know when the devil lies to me. Lead me away from his lies and toward Your truth. Amen.

BIG, FAT LIES

O Lord, save me from lying lips and a false tongue.
PSALM 120:2

Maybe you've played a game where someone begins a story and other players add to it. "There was a girl at my school." "There was a girl at my school, and she had big, green eyes." "There was a girl at my school, and she had big, green eyes, and they never closed." "There was a girl at my school, and she had big, green eyes, and they never closed, and she was an alien!"

Games where you make up stories and exaggerate the truth can be fun. But when you aren't playing a game, God wants you to always be truthful. If you make up stories or exaggerate the truth by adding things that didn't really happen, then you are telling lies—big, fat lies.

God wants you to tell the truth. If you lie, you might feel guilty. That's God's way of reminding you to examine your behavior.

Dear God, I know Better than to make up stories and exaggerate the truth. If ever I feel like telling lies, remind me to Be truthful. Amen.

WHERE AM I GOING?

The steps of a good man are led by the Lord.
And He is happy in his way. When he falls, he will not
be thrown down, because the Lord holds his hand.
PSALM 37:23–24

You are on an amazing journey—a journey called life. Life is an adventure, and you are just beginning your travels.

So where are you going? That's a mystery. Only God knows. What you can be sure of, though, is God will lead you. There will be some bumps along the way. Sometimes you will mess up, trip, and fall. But don't worry! God has you by the hand. He will help you to get up, brush yourself off, and keep going.

You can't see too far ahead. But you can set small goals that keep you moving forward, goals you are pretty sure you can reach. One goal leads to the next and the next, and it's those goals that keep you moving through life. What is one new goal you can set for yourself today? Make it something you know you can accomplish.

Lord God, together we're on this lifelong adventure. I'm grateful You're leading the way. Amen.

BUMPS AND BRUISES

We think of those who stayed true to Him as happy even though they suffered. You have heard how long Job waited. You have seen what the Lord did for him in the end. The Lord is full of loving-kindness and pity.

JAMES 5:11

The Bible tells of a man named Job who was living a great life. But then his life began falling apart. Almost every bad thing you could imagine happened to Job. Still, he refused to stop believing God would help him pick up the pieces and keep moving forward. God did just that! It took some time, but God mended what was wrong, and He blessed Job with a good, happy, and very long life.

No one lives an absolutely perfect life. Yours will cause you some bumps and bruises along the way. But if you stay true to God and have faith in His loving-kindness, He will give you the courage and strength to keep moving forward.

Dear God, when You made me, You promised never to leave me. When life gets hard, please remind me You are still with me and helping me. Amen.

I WILL PERSEVERE

*Let your eyes look straight in front of you, and
keep looking at what is in front of you. Watch the
path of your feet, and all your ways will be sure.*

PROVERBS 4:25–26

The word *persevere* means to keep going even when things
get tough. The Bible has many stories of people who kept
going when life got hard.

When God created you, He made you to be like those
people. He gave you the ability to be courageous and
strong and to trust that He will lead you out of whatever
trouble you are in.

Eyes forward all the time! If you stop and do nothing,
you will be stuck in your trouble. But if you keep moving
carefully, watching your steps along the way, you will
eventually leave your trouble behind. You were made to
persevere, to say "I can" when you think you can't, and to
believe that God will give you some of His power to keep
you moving forward.

Dear God, when I meet trouble on my life
journey, I will trust You to give me strength
and courage to persevere. Amen.

I WILL SET BOUNDARIES

Thorns and traps are in the way of the sinful.
He who watches himself will stay far from them.

PROVERBS 22:5

A boundary is an imaginary line that separates two things, often something good from something bad. Imagine you are hiking through thick woods. You're trying to find your way with no clear path. It would be wise to keep your eyes open for hunters' traps and bushes with thorns. You'd want to stay away from them and limit yourself to walking where it's safe. You would set an imaginary boundary between yourself and those places where you might get hurt.

On your life journey, God will help you identify places, or people's behavior, that might harm you. Once you've identified them, you can set imaginary boundaries so you don't cross into those places. Can you think of a few boundaries you've set for yourself? What is something you won't do because it might cause you harm?

Dear God, I know You want me to set Boundaries when things feel unsafe. Help me to identify the people, places, and things I should stay away from. Amen.

149

I WILL SAY NO

"Let your yes be YES. Let your no be NO."
MATTHEW 5:37

God has given you the ability to know right from wrong, good from bad, safe from unsafe, and healthy from unhealthy. If on your life journey you forget what's right, good, safe, or healthy, you will sense God saying inside your heart, "No!" Listen to His voice. Get back on the path He wants you to walk.

Some people may try to lead you in the wrong direction. It's okay to say no to them. In fact, you *should* say no. God doesn't want you pulled away from Him. Some people are afraid they won't be liked or accepted if they say no. Don't let that be you. Never follow those who lead you away from God.

Stay near to Him even if it means others will turn against you. Do you remember a time you said no to something you knew was wrong?

Heavenly Father, if someone tries to lead me away from You, give me the strength and courage to say no. Amen.

I WILL TRY TO GET ALONG

I ask you with all my heart in the name of the
Lord Jesus Christ to agree among yourselves.
Do not be divided into little groups. Think
and act as if you all had the same mind.
1 CORINTHIANS 1:10

God didn't create you to walk through life alone. You will meet many people along the way, all kinds of people. Some you will have a lot in common with; others you won't. But don't turn away from those who are different. You could learn and grow the most from knowing them.

Instead of walking through life with only a small group of family members and friends, welcome others to walk along with you. And if there are disagreements among you, do your best to work them out. Do your best to listen to others too. Be understanding, caring, and forgiving. Always set the best example of how God wants His people to behave, and do your best to lead others toward Him.

Dear God, I wonder who I will meet on this life journey. Help me to welcome new friends and to try my best to get along with everyone. Amen.

151

I WILL TAKE RESPONSIBILITY

*It will not go well for the man who hides
his sins, but he who tells his sins and turns
from them will be given loving-pity.*
PROVERBS 28:13

God made you with a conscience, an inner voice that tells you right from wrong. It's God's voice, His Spirit speaking to you.

As you go through life, you will mess up—we all do! When you make a mistake, you have a choice. You can hide what you've done, or you can take responsibility. Taking responsibility means listening to God's voice and being willing to say, "I made a mistake" or "What I did was wrong." It means asking others for forgiveness and asking God to forgive you too.

You might be able to hide your mess-ups from others, but you can't hide them from God. It can be hard to admit you were wrong, but you will earn respect when you admit your mistakes. Think of a time you took responsibility. How did it make you feel?

Dear God, remind me to listen to Your voice and admit when I'm wrong. I don't want to be shy about taking responsibility for my actions and my words. Amen.

I WILL LOOK FOR GOD'S BLESSINGS

The Lord has done great things for us and we are glad.
PSALM 126:3

Some days it's difficult to dig up gladness. Imagine you're having a bad day. It begins when you get up late and miss the school bus. In class you don't do well on a pop quiz. Then the school lunch menu offers your least favorite things. After school you miss a goal at your soccer match and your team loses. If that were you, you'd probably end your day not feeling glad.

But if you had looked for God's blessings in the middle of your messy day, you would have found them. And if you concentrated more on His blessings than on what went wrong, you would have discovered some of the gladness God puts inside your heart. Not every day on your life journey will be a good day, but if you keep your mind on God, every day will be a *blessed* day.

Father, whenever I have a Bad day, I will remind myself to look for Your Blessings. Amen.

I WILL STAY POSITIVE

Let your minds and hearts be made new.
EPHESIANS 4:23

Have you ever heard someone say, "Look on the bright side"? That means having a positive attitude, which often means turning around the way you think.

God wants you to think of whatever is good and worth giving thanks for (Philippians 4:8). When your thinking turns negative, you can turn it around by finding something good to think about. What if you sprained your ankle at dance class and you couldn't participate for two weeks? That could make you feel gloomy because your recital is coming soon and you need to practice. How could you turn your thinking in a more positive direction? You could be glad you didn't break your ankle. You could look forward to dancing again. You could be grateful you have family at home helping you to heal and feel better.

Give it a try: How could you think positively if your dad had to work when he promised to take you to the movies?

Dear God, help me to look on the bright side even when I'm feeling down. Amen.

I WILL MAKE TIME FOR ME

In the morning before the sun was up, Jesus went to a place where He could be alone. He prayed there.
MARK 1:35

As you walk through life, you will have days when you just don't feel like doing anything. You will want the world to stop spinning all around you. You will want people to leave you alone for a while. That's okay. We all feel like that sometimes.

God made you—and everyone else—to take a little time off when needed. God rested after He created the earth and the sky and everything in them (Genesis 2:2). Jesus had times when He wanted to be alone too. He went to a quiet place and talked with God. You don't have to rush through life every day or race toward meeting your goals.

Life is a long journey, and sometimes you need time to rest. If you could go anywhere at all to be alone and rest for a while, where would you go? What would you do to feel refreshed?

Lord God, on days when I feel grumpy and I want to be left alone, I will find a quiet place to rest and be with You. Amen.

I WILL LEARN SOMETHING NEW

I will show you and teach you in the way you should go. I will tell you what to do with My eye upon you.
PSALM 32:8

Think of all the new things you've learned recently. In school you learned new skills that will help you become even better at reading, math, and science. You might have learned something about the world's history and its people. As you've read this book and your Bible, you've learned more about God and Jesus, and you've learned new things about yourself too.

Every day you are learning and growing. The knowledge you store in your head and your heart is important. God promised to lead you and teach you in the way you should go. At the end of each day, think about what you have learned. Ask God to help you use it. What you learn in school will help you find a job someday and succeed in your work. What you learn about life will help make you wise.

Dear God, please give me a desire to learn. Then show me and teach me in the way I should go. Amen.

I WILL READ MY BIBLE

*All the Holy Writings are God-given and are made
alive by Him. Man is helped when he is taught God's
Word. It shows what is wrong. It changes the way of
a man's life. It shows him how to be right with God.*
2 TIMOTHY 3:16

Just as God put it in your heart to listen to His words, He
put it in the hearts of men to write His words down. God
chose the writers, and their writings make up the Bible. God
wants people to read and think about His words.

God speaks to us through the Bible. His words teach us
what is right and wrong, and they help us. If you read your
Bible and obey God's words, it will change the way you live.
You will learn that God loves you. You will discover you can
trust Him to be your helper and life partner. You will even get
a glimpse of what it's like to live with Him in heaven someday.

Get in the habit of reading your Bible and thinking
about its words.

Thank you for the Bible, God. I will read it
every day and learn more about You. Amen.

I WILL PRAY MORE

You must pray at all times as the Holy Spirit leads you to pray. Pray for the things that are needed. You must watch and keep on praying. Remember to pray for all Christians.
EPHESIANS 6:18

Do you say prayers only at bedtime and maybe before you eat? God made you to communicate with Him all the time and not just at certain times during the day.

When God wants to hear from you, you might feel Him inside your heart encouraging you to talk with Him. He wants you to pray for everything you need, especially big things like needing to feel loved, accepted, forgiven, or safe. He wants you to tell Him your thoughts, ask questions, and seek His guidance. God wants you to keep on praying.

You can pray to Him aloud or silently through your thoughts. Get in the habit of praying all the time. If you can't think of what to pray about, pray for others. Ask God to help with whatever they need.

Dear God, I will do my best to pray more often. If I forget, please remind me. Amen.

I WILL PUT GOD FIRST

But more than anything else, put God's work first and do what he wants. Then the other things will be yours as well.
MATTHEW 6:33 CEV

God said, "Do not worship any god except me" (Exodus 20:3 CEV). God created you to worship Him, and He wants to come first in your life.

You don't have to wait in line for God's attention; it's always there for you. He has the amazing ability to put you and each of His children first every time. Jesus said if you put your relationship with God first, then everything else will fall into place.

Be on the lookout, though. Other gods will try to get between you and the one true God. A god is anything you make more important than God your heavenly Father. If you had to choose between God and your friends, which would you choose? If God asked you to choose between helping with an event at church or eating pizza and watching a movie, what would you do?

Dear God. I want to put You first in my life. Help me to recognize other gods that try to get in the way. Amen.

159

I WILL SERVE OTHERS

*God. . .will not forget your work and the love
you have shown him as you have helped
his people and continue to help them.*
HEBREWS 6:10 NIV

God made you to do His work, and He will never forget what you've done for Him.

Imagine you get to heaven someday and Jesus says to you, "I was hungry and you gave Me food to eat. I was thirsty and you gave Me water to drink. I was a stranger and you gave Me a room. I had no clothes and you gave Me clothes to wear. I was sick and you cared for Me. I was in prison and you came to see Me" (Matthew 25:35–36). You answer, "But, Jesus, I've never done those things for You." The truth is if you gave food and water to people in need, donated clothing, welcomed new friends, cared for the sick, or helped others through their trouble, it was as if you were doing those things for Jesus. You were serving Him by serving others here on earth.

Dear Jesus. I want to help You By serving others. Show me what I can do. Amen.

I WILL WORSHIP GOD

Come, let us bow down in worship. Let us get down on our knees before the Lord Who made us.

PSALM 95:6

God, your Creator, does great things for you. He creates your every breath, every beat of your heart, and every step you take. He blesses you with food, clothing, a place to live, family, friends, pets, teachers. . .the list of how God blesses and helps you is endless.

God made you to worship Him. The word *worship* means showing God through words and actions that you think He is awesome. You worship God in prayer by telling Him you love Him. You worship Him by singing praise songs and also by looking for the small things He does for you every day and appreciating them. Most of all, you worship God by saying, "Thank You."

When you pray tonight, get down on your knees and worship your heavenly Father. Thank Him for making you and leading you through life.

Father God. You are so wonderful. I appreciate all You do for me. I love You. I praise You. and I thank You for Your many Blessings. Amen.

I WILL BE GRATEFUL

The LORD forgives our sins, heals us when we are
sick, and protects us from death. His kindness
and love are a crown on our heads. Each day
that we live, he provides for our needs and
gives us the strength of a young eagle.
PSALM 103:3–5 CEV

When God made you, He planned to bless you in many different ways. Read Psalm 103:3–5 again. It lists several ways God blesses us. He gives us so much to be thankful for! Think about the ways God has blessed you as you answer these questions:

- What does gratefulness mean to you?
- Do you think it's important to be grateful? Why?
- Can you name three people you are grateful for?
- What are you most thankful for?
- When was the last time you said, "Thank you"?
- How often do you thank God for His blessings?

The more you think about gratefulness, the more thankful you will be. Give it a try today. Look for reasons to say thank you. Then count how many times you said it.

Lord, please open my eyes to even more
things to be grateful for. Amen.

WITH ALL MY HEART

O Lord my God, I will give thanks to You with all my heart. I will bring honor to Your name forever.
PSALM 86:12

God made you to notice the good things He does and to be grateful. When He created your heart, the invisible heart that makes you YOU, He made it capable of holding tons of gratitude for the many ways He blesses you.

Look for ways God has blessed you so you can learn to be thankful in all things (1 Thessalonians 5:18). One way to release your gratitude is simply to pray and thank God for His goodness. Telling Him you are grateful is important. It is also important to show Him you are grateful. You can show God you've noticed His blessings by keeping a journal where every day you write down what you are thankful for. You can also show you are grateful by telling others about how God has blessed you.

Can you think of more ways to thank God for being so good and caring toward you? Be grateful to Him with all your heart.

. . . .

Dear God, show me how I can be thankful to You with my whole heart. Amen.

HIDDEN BLESSINGS

Everything God made is good. We should not put anything aside if we can take it and thank God for it.
1 TIMOTHY 4:4

Do you enjoy searching for hidden objects? Here's an activity to try. From morning to night, look for God's hidden blessings all around you, things that bring you joy.

Maybe you woke up this morning to the scent of your favorite breakfast. Pancakes! A blessing. While waiting for your mom to drive you to school, you saw a colorful bird, one like you've never seen. Another blessing. On the car radio, you heard a cool new song from your favorite performer. Blessing! Your dad picked you up after school and took you out for ice cream. Double blessing—time spent with Dad and a tasty treat. And when you got home, your dog rushed to greet you, looking for a hug and some love. Blessing.

God made you with five senses, (sight, sound, scent, taste, and touch) to experience the world around you. Use your senses all day long as you search for His hidden treasures.

Dear God, every day, all day, I see Your Blessings all around me. Amen.

KIND BLESSINGS

Let them give thanks to the Lord for His loving-kindness and His great works to the children of men!
PSALM 107:21

Family members, friends, teachers, coaches, pastors, police officers, paramedics. . . God uses people to bless us. You can think of these helpers as God's angels doing His work here on earth. They're not really angels, but God uses them to spread His loving-kindness around.

God wants you to notice and to thank those who bless you. If you got hurt and broke a bone, paramedics, doctors, and nurses would help you. You could tell them, "Thank you. You are a blessing!" If a strap on your backpack broke and your teacher used tape to temporarily fix it, you could say, "Thank you! That was a blessing." When God leads others to help you, He is using them to show you His loving-kindness. Remember to say thank you to those who help, and thank God for them too.

Heavenly Father, I'm grateful for the people You send to bless me with kindness and help. I will let them know I appreciate them by always saying "Thank you." Amen.

EARTH AND SKY

"O Lord God! See, You have made the heavens and the earth by Your great power and by Your long arm! Nothing is too hard for You!"
JEREMIAH 32:17

What is your favorite thing to see in the sky? Do you love watching fluffy, white clouds changing shape? After a storm, do you rush outside looking for a rainbow? You might be a star gazer searching the night sky for constellations and planets, hoping to see a shooting star or maybe the northern lights.

Are you a woodsy girl who would love camping and exploring new trails, or would you rather be by the ocean looking for small sea animals and shells on the beach?

God made you to be in awe of what He has made and to be grateful for His creations. The earth and sky hold so many wonders. Have you noticed how with each season things change? God, in His magnificence, always gives us new things to notice and be grateful for.

Dear God, thank You for making me aware of the wonders of the earth and sky. Thank You for all Your creations. Amen.

KING OF ALL KINGS

Let us come before Him giving thanks. Let us make a sound of joy to Him with songs. For the Lord is a great God, and a great King above all gods.
PSALM 95:2–3

God created you to be grateful that He is the one and only God. The Bible calls Him King of all kings. No one can match God's power over earth and all His creation. So much about Him is too great for our human minds to understand. God wants us to be grateful to Him for being our God, for being so great, wonderful, loving, and kind that His goodness is beyond our understanding.

From the beginning of time, people have come to God with thanksgiving. They have expressed their thankfulness with songs. The Bible says there will come a day when every living thing in heaven, on the earth, under the earth, and in the sea will thank God and honor Him (Revelation 5:13). Make time today to thank God for just being God, your Creator, the King of all kings.

Lord God. I'm grateful to You for being my King. the one-and-only. all-powerful God. Amen.

ENDLESS LOVE

*Give thanks to the LORD, for he is
good; his love endures forever.*
PSALM 106:1 NIV

God created you with love. When He made you, God planned for you to love Him forever and to be grateful for His love.

God loves everything—and everyone—that He made. He cares deeply about His creation, especially people. That's why He sent Jesus to die on the cross and take the punishment for sin. When you accept that wonderful gift, You become His adopted daughter—and He will never stop loving you. Even if you mess up many times and even if you turn away from Him for a while, God will love you as if you were the only person on earth.

God's love for you is endless. He loved you when He made you, He loves you just as you are, and when you get to heaven someday God will love you there *forever*.

Dear God, thank You for loving me!
Thank You for loving me in a special way
with Your perfect, endless love. Amen.

WISDOM AND STRENGTH

"I give thanks and praise to You, O God of my fathers.
For You have given me wisdom and power."
DANIEL 2:23

What are some difficult decisions you've had to make? Maybe you decided to end a friendship with someone. Or maybe a girl at school said something unkind to you, and instead of walking away you decided to stand up for yourself. As you get older, you will face many important decisions, life-changing decisions about your education, who to date, who you will marry, your job. . . God created you to make wise choices and to be strong enough to do what's right even when it's hard.

If you ask Him to guide you, He will help you to choose. When you and God decide together what is right, He will give you power to act on your decisions and carry them out. Remember to thank God for making you wise and strong, not just today but all through your life.

Dear God, thank You for providing me with wisdom and strength. Throughout my life I will trust in Your guidance and Be grateful for Your help. Amen.

THE BIG MEETING

I will give You thanks in the big meeting.
I will praise You among many people.
PSALM 35:18

In Psalm 35, King David says he will thank God in "the big meeting" and praise Him among many people. Today, we think of the big meeting as church. It's where Christians meet each week to learn more about God and praise and thank Him. God's churches are all over the world. It pleases Him to see His people meeting together. Their praises are like music to His ears.

Do you go to church? It's a great place to meet new friends. Most churches have fun activities for girls your age. As you learn with your friends about Jesus, you will grow stronger in your faith. God wants you to make friends with other Christians. He wants all His people to gather together to worship Him and thank Him for the wonderful things He does.

If you don't have a church, maybe one of your girlfriends does. Ask if you can go with her sometime.

Heavenly Father, I thank You for my church and all my Christian friends. Amen.

SPECIAL PEOPLE

I always thank God when I speak of you in my prayers.
PHILEMON 4

Have you been keeping a list of what you are grateful for? Let's add more people to that list. When God made you, He planned a whole army of people to help and guide you.

Who in your family, other than your parents, gives good advice? What teacher has made the biggest difference in your life? Which of your friends can you always count on? Who made you feel welcome when you felt all alone? Who will love you even when you mess up? Who gave up something to spend time with you? Who helped you solve a problem? Who makes you feel safe? Who helped you become even better at doing something you love? Who makes you feel really good about yourself?

When you say your prayers, remember the special people in your life and thank God for them.

Dear God, You have put good people
in my life to help and guide me.
Thank You for every one of them. Amen.

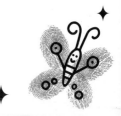

THANK YOU FOR ME!

*Know that the Lord is God. It is He Who
made us, and not we ourselves. We are
His people and the sheep of His field.*
PSALM 100:3

Check your gratitude list one more time and see if *you're* on it. If not, add yourself to that list!

God, the Creator of the earth, sky, and universe, decided to make you. He took great care when making you. He created you just the way He wanted you to be. God made you with a purpose—to serve Him by helping with His work here on earth.

God didn't just create you and forget about you. He made you His ongoing work in progress. He's not done with you yet. With each new experience, God is teaching you about life. His teaching will go on every day for as long as you live; and as you learn and grow, if you ask God to guide you, He will use you to serve Him.

So, thank God for YOU, God's servant.

Thank You, God, for creating me and
giving me life. I look forward to
serving You every day. Amen.

SHARE WHAT YOU HAVE

*God will give you enough so you can always
give to others. Then many will give thanks
to God for sending gifts through us.*
2 CORINTHIANS 9:11

God has made you aware of many things to be grateful for. When you think about how He has blessed you, look around and notice others who could use some blessings. God made you to share what you have.

No matter how much or how little you have, God gives you enough to share. That doesn't mean you must always give money, food, clothing, and other needed things. You can also share what you have with others by using the special qualities that make you YOU. You can share your special way of comforting people when they are sad, or notice and help someone with a chore, or use one of your skills to teach someone.

You can do something more. When people thank you, tell them to thank God too—because it was Him who led you to help.

Dear God, thank you for giving me enough
to share. Thank you for reminding me
to share my blessings. Amen.

EYES LIKE JESUS'

*He did not need anyone to tell Him about
man. He knew what was in man.*
JOHN 2:25

God gave you Jesus as the perfect example of someone who noticed and helped those in need. No one had to tell Jesus how to help. He always saw, and He knew what to do.

Do you have eyes like Jesus? Do you have eyes that see when someone needs help? God wants you to pay attention to what's inside the hearts of others and recognize what they need. Often you can tell what's in someone's heart by how they behave. Do they seem sad, angry, frustrated, scared? You've had those same feelings inside your heart, and that should give you some ideas of how you can help.

Being aware of how people feel is a first step in knowing how to serve them. If you aren't sure what to do, you can always ask Jesus to show you.

Dear Jesus, I want to be more like You and notice when others need help. Open my eyes to their needs and show me what to do. Amen.

I SPY

"In every way I showed you that by working hard like this we can help those who are weak. We must remember what the Lord Jesus said, 'We are more happy when we give than when we receive.'"

ACTS 20:35

God gave you eyes to see with. Now put them to work.

When you are around other kids, see if you can spy those who need help. You've likely needed the same kind of help, so think about how you can serve them. Then put your thoughts into action. If you spy someone new at school who looks like they're lost, ask if you can help with directions. If you spy someone looking like they need a friend, say hello and talk for a while. Maybe you'll see someone needing help with something you are good at. Lend a hand.

When you become better at noticing what others need, God will give you ideas about how you can serve them. And when you serve them, you should be happy because you are serving God too!

. . . .

Dear God, it makes me happy when I can help others. I think it makes You happy too! Amen.

CLEAN IT UP

*"And I brought you into a rich land to
eat its fruit and its good things. But you
came and made My land unclean."*
JEREMIAH 2:7

God gave you the earth, and He made you to care for it.
You probably see things happening every day that make
the earth unclean. You can help change that.

Start by picking up trash. Learn the best way to get rid
of it. Your city or town will likely have a web page that tells
you what to do. Whenever you can, use reusable containers. Avoid cups, plates, and utensils that get thrown away.
Don't waste food; take only what you need. Recycle things.
See if you can find new uses for what you might otherwise
throw away. Instead of trashing something when it's broken,
decide if it can be fixed.

These are just some of the things you could do. Can you
think of others? Remember, caring for the earth is caring
for God's creation. It's another way of serving Him and
showing Him you care.

Dear God, thank You for planet Earth.
Guide me to love it and care for it. Amen.

OLD PEOPLE

*"Even when you are old I will be the same.
And even when your hair turns white, I will
help you. I will take care of what I have made.
I will carry you, and will save you."*

ISAIAH 46:4

What do you see when you look at old people? Wrinkles? White hair? That's not what God sees. He sees the inner hearts of those precious children He made. He cares for them when they are old just as much as He did the day He created them.

When you look at old people, try to see them with God's eyes. You can serve them (and God) by helping with things the older persons' bodies can't do well anymore: carrying a heavy object; cutting grass, raking leaves, and other yard work; taking their dog for a walk. . . You can also help by showing them how to use electronics and new inventions they might not be familiar with.

God made you to serve everyone, young and old. Keep your eyes open for those who might need you.

Heavenly Father, make me aware of the older people in my life and show me how to serve them. Amen.

LITTLE ONES

"When you welcome even a child because of me, you welcome me."

MARK 9:37 CEV

You were a little kid once. You probably remember what it felt like to be very young. You didn't know many things and wondered about them.

Do you know God made you to be a teacher to those younger than you? He wants all of us to share our wisdom and experience with those who are younger and learning. Maybe you have younger siblings. If you are patient with them and help them to learn, you will serve them by being God's helper. When you teach little kids to be kind, caring, and respectful, you lead them to become more like Jesus.

Jesus said when we welcome children into our lives, it is like we are welcoming Him. What can you teach younger children about Jesus? How do you think knowing about Jesus will help them as they get older?

Dear Jesus, I want to set a good example for the younger kids in my life. Guide me to teach them not only how to do things, but also to know and love You. Amen.

I WILL DO GOOD

Do not let yourselves get tired of doing good.
If we do not give up, we will get what is coming
to us at the right time. Because of this, we
should do good to everyone. For sure, we should
do good to those who belong to Christ.
GALATIANS 6:9–10

The world is filled with people, and every one of them needs something. You can't save the world all by yourself, but you can do your part by looking for ways to spread God's goodness around.

God made you to do good to everyone. It doesn't have to be some grand act of goodness. It can be little things like being polite and respectful, holding the door open for someone, writing a thank-you note, or giving a compliment.

When we are good to each other, we serve God by making the world a better place. Some people will notice the good things you do, others won't. Don't become tired of doing good because of those who don't notice. God sees, and that is enough.

Dear God, help me to do good to everyone I meet whether they appreciate it or not. Amen.

MY COMMUNITY

*See, how good and how pleasing it is for
brothers to live together as one!*
PSALM 133:1

God made you to be part of a community. Wherever you live, whether it's a big city, a small town, or something in between, you share that space with others.

Your community is a great place to practice serving others and serving God. You can do things like donate clothing you've outgrown, make cards for residents at nursing homes, read to younger children or, if you are old enough, you can babysit. You can serve in bigger ways too. Get your family involved. Help out at a local food bank. Take a treat to first responders to thank them for their service. Volunteer to help with events at church. Learn CPR. Deliver a meal to someone who's sick. Have a garage sale and donate the money to a charity.

Make a list of how you can help. Write down what you can do by yourself, with your friends, and with your family.

Dear God, I want to serve You and my community.
Please guide me. Show me how I can help. Amen.

WORKING TOGETHER

"For where two or three are gathered together in My name, there I am with them."

MATTHEW 18:20

God created you as one of His many helpers. In the Bible you'll often see God's people working together to serve Him. People working together can accomplish great things.

You can serve God and do His work by joining a club, group, or other organization that has a specific goal or purpose. The purpose might be to raise money for a cause or to volunteer your time, talents, and skills. It could be to hold a vacation Bible school, clean up the earth, organize a food drive, or assemble care packages. When you do these things in Jesus' name, so that others can know Him, everyone wins!

Working with others for a purpose is a great way to make friends who share your willingness to help. Jesus said where His followers are gathered together, He is with them. Ask Jesus to lead you. You can find groups to join in your community, at school, and at church. Look for those who serve God by doing something good.

Dear Jesus, I want to join with others to do God's work. Lead me to a group with a purpose. Amen.

ALL GOD'S CREATURES

A man who is right with God cares for his animal.
PROVERBS 12:10

When you read your Bible, you will see that God made Adam, the first human, to be head over all the animals (Genesis 1:26). From the beginning, humans have been responsible for caring for God's creatures here on earth.

God made you to care for them too. Taking care of animals is another way to serve God. He knows every animal He has created. Jesus said not even one bird falls to the earth without God knowing (Matthew 10:29). If God cares so much for His animals, then you should too.

If you have pets, it is your job to take good care of them. You can also care for wild animals and birds by providing them with shelter and food. Read about the wild animals in your area and learn how to help them. You can contact your local animal shelters to find out how you can help with the animals there too. Everything God made is important to Him. He remembers and cares for all His creations.

Lord God, I will treat Your animals with kindness and do my best to care for them. Amen.

THE MOST IMPORTANT SHARE

I am not ashamed of the Good News. It is the power of God. It is the way He saves men from the punishment of their sins if they put their trust in Him.
ROMANS 1:16

You have been learning to serve God by sharing with others what you have and who you are. You are giving them the best of what makes you YOU.

What's the most important thing to share? It's your relationship with God and Jesus!

God made you to share the good news about who He is and all the wonderful things He does. He made you to share that His Son, Jesus, came to earth to take the punishment for people's sins so they could live forever in heaven.

Tell your friends about God and Jesus. If some don't believe you or make fun of you for sharing, don't let that stop you. God is always listening and watching. He will use what you share to draw others nearer to Him. You are God's servant—His helper—and that's a wonderful thing to be.

God, I will never be ashamed to share the good news of Jesus with others. Amen.

WHEN GOD SEES ME

For if a man belongs to Christ, he is a new person.
The old life is gone. New life has begun.
2 CORINTHIANS 5:17

God sees you. When He sees you, He sees what's inside your heart. He sees your behavior. He sees how you get along with others. He is always watching over you, helping you to learn, grow, and become more like Him.

In the beginning, when God created the sky, the earth, and everything in it, He decided it was good. When He created you, God looked at you and decided you were good too. He celebrates you. All of heaven celebrates if you choose to follow Jesus.

Accepting Him as your Savior gives you a clean heart and takes away any sin that's in there. It makes your heart like new. When God looks at you, He sees His beautiful girl. You are beautiful in His sight right now, and you always will be.

Dear God, when You look into my heart, You see all that I am. You've made me unique and special. I love who I am, and I love You too. Amen.

THE BEST THING ABOUT ME

*I pray that you will be able to understand how wide
and how long and how high and how deep His love is.*
EPHESIANS 3:18

You are God's creation, a wonderful mixture of personality traits, special talents, and skills. What is the best thing about you? That might be a hard question to answer.

You've discovered so many amazing things about yourself. But the best thing about you is that you are God's love! Maybe your mom, dad, or grandma has called you their love. God says you are His love every day. Each day He demonstrates His love for you.

God's love is special because it's His perfect one-of-a-kind forever love. The Bible says God is love and everything about Him is loving. He made you with love, and you are a part of His family. God made you to be like Himself and to share His love with others. God's love for you is bigger and deeper and wider than you can ever imagine or understand.

Girl—don't ever forget this—you are *so* loved!

Oh God, help me to see myself as that
special girl You created. Thank You
for making me ME! Amen.

WHAT'S NEXT?

*Teach me the way I should go for
I lift up my soul to You.*
PSALM 143:8

Only God knows what's in your future. But you can imagine and talk with God about it. Here are some things to think about:

What job do you see yourself doing when you grow up? Would you like to get married someday? Is there a new skill you want to learn? Would you like to travel? Where do you want to go? Is there a physical challenge you would like to accomplish, like running a marathon or learning a new sport? Is there something you would like to change about yourself? How would you like your relationship with God to grow in the future—to have more faith or pray more often?

Ask God to teach you the way you should go. You can trust Him to lead and guide you.

Dear God, lead me into the future. Show me the way to go. You created me. You love me, and I trust You to guide me all the days of my life. Amen.

SCRIPTURE INDEX

MORE GREAT DEVOTIONS FOR GIRLS!

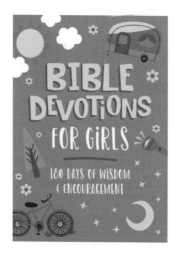

This deeply encouraging devotional is inspired by the words of Jesus in the New Testament. From His teaching and preaching to Jesus' miracles and parables, you'll read the life-changing, memorable truths of Christ alongside a relevant devotion guaranteed to motivate and challenge you to grow in your faith.

Paperback / ISBN 978-1-63609-684-1

Find This and More from Barbour
Publishing at Your Favorite Bookstore
or www.barbourbooks.com

BARBOUR
PUBLISHING